Home Is Where the Boat Is

Emy Thomas

ISBN: 1-4107-7283-7 (e-book)
ISBN: 1-4107-7282-9 (Paperback)

Library of Congress Catalog Card Number: 93-94005

This book is printed on acid free paper.

Printed in the United States of America.

Illustrations by Cynthia Hatfield.

1stBooks - rev. 09/26/03

Also by Emy Thomas

Non-fiction

Life in the Left Lane

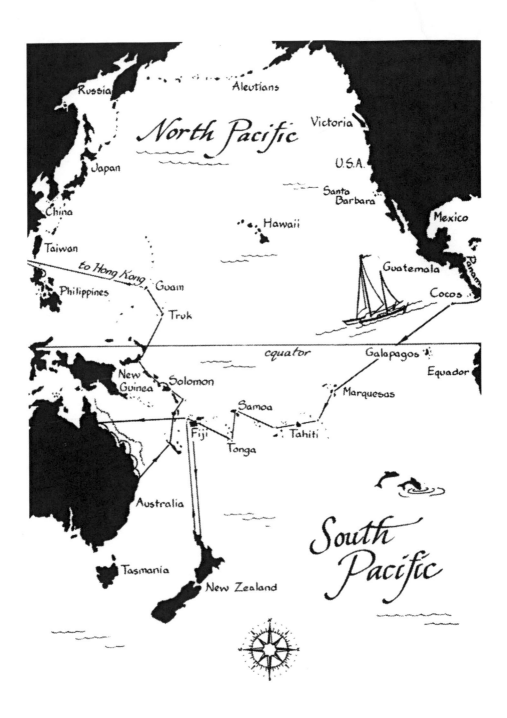

Russia
Aleutians
North Pacific
Victoria
Japan
U.S.A.
China
Santa Barbara
Taiwan
Hawaii
Mexico
to Hong Kong
Guatemala
Guam
Philippines
Cocos
Panama
Truk
equator
Galapagos
Equador
New Guinea
Solomon
Marquesas
Samoa
Fiji
Tahiti
Tonga
Australia
Tasmania
New Zealand
South Pacific

DEDICATION

To my mother,

Catherine ("Kitty") McGeary Thomas Chamberlain

ACKNOWLEDGMENTS

The author wishes to thank:

Connie Underhill, my editor and friend.

Jim Fairbank and Betty Fairbank Griggs, who introduced me to the cruising scene.

And all those others who supported me and this book in one way or another, including especially Nancy and Simon Scott, Bob Friedman, Joe Gribbins, Tom and Joan Thomas, Bob Thomas, Tinker Bell Riggs, Eunice Trowbridge, Irene ("Queenie") Cerqueira, William Kennedy, Peter Reeves, Betsy Chamberlain, Kent Ellis, Maradee Abbott, Harry Abbott, Hope Kobak, Valerie Rout, Betty and Comrie Watt, Chambie and Barb Ferry, Helen Scott-Harman, Bob Carpenter, the Late Ginny Low, Candia Atwater, Evelyn Grant, Manon Lu Christ, Maggie Foster and Erica Smilowitz.

TABLE OF CONTENTS

SAILING AWAY

ON ALL THE OCEANS of the world, there is a small but ever-growing subculture of adventurous men and women who are cruising around in small boats. They have sailed away from their "real" lives, maybe forever, to live a dream.

They island hop through the Caribbean, cross the Pacific Ocean or circumnavigate the world, going where they please when they please. They are free.

They are known in America as boat bums, boat people, boaters, cruisers, sailors, yachtsmen. In British Commonwealth countries they are called "yachties," just as bikers are called "bikies" and surfers "surfies." The slang recognizes a commitment, a lifestyle.

Not every sailor becomes a yachtie. Of the many who dream of pulling up stakes and sailing away into the sunset, few have the dedication or self-sufficiency required to actually pull it off.

Financial independence is not, surprisingly, an essential prerequisite. Practical knowledge is, the more the better. A do-it-yourself-jack-of-all-trades-and-fix-it-man is the one most likely to succeed as a yachtie. He can deal with the myriad problems yachts are subject to and, if necessary, he can finance his travels by picking up odd jobs along the way.

I was privileged to share a dozen years of cruising with Peter Hansen, an Englishman, who was the epitome of a cruising yachtie: independent, handy and resourceful, confident, cheerful, relaxed and poor. For him, wandering was a way of life, and home was where the boat was.

I met Peter in Tortola, in the British Virgin Islands, shortly after he crossed the Atlantic with two hitchhikers, novice sailors, as crew. He was patching up his boat. I soon discovered that he was always patching up his boat, but for Peter, keeping *Solanderi* seaworthy was an enduring labor of love. A homemade plywood catamaran, she was not the most desirable cruising yacht, perhaps, but she was all he could afford and he had the enthusiasm and ingenuity required to keep her afloat and mobile.

I was fascinated by his accomplishments and charmed by his playful and gentle manner, but I thought he was a loser, because I was counting things. His world consisted of a boat in need of major repairs, a few scruffy articles of clothing, some books, a bunch of rusty hand tools, a couple of boxes of food, a case of rum, a dog and a few crumpled dollars in his pocket.

Peter, in his quiet way, helped me appreciate other standards of success. As a dedicated "gypsea," he had everything he wanted: a boat, the expertise to make it work and the freedom to enjoy it. He was a happy and contented man, and I luckily had the time and sense to enjoy him.

I was on an open-end vacation, a burned-out journalist wondering what to do next. Going to sea in a small sailboat with a penniless man was not one of the possibilities that had crossed my mind. A middle-class American, almost 40, I had done some unconventional things in my life, but I was not a sailor, I had never considered "dropping out," and I had never heard of yachties.

I had no intention of becoming one and sailing halfway around the world when I moved aboard Peter's boat, but one beautiful island led to another, and I was in love.

We wandered all over the Caribbean and Pacific for 13 mostly idyllic years. I developed a love-hate relationship with sailing that was directly linked to the weather. When the sun was shining and the sea was sparkling and mild, I thought it was a glorious life. But when the world went gray and the ocean turned nasty, I felt it was a stupid, masochistic thing to do. I was afraid in rough weather, and since the chances of poor conditions were about 50-50 in the open ocean, I secretly dreaded it every time we went to sea. But I wasn't going to let Peter sail away without me.

I was a reluctant sailor but I loved being in port, and fortunately even the most ardent cruisers spend about 90 percent of their time anchored. Then I loved the cruising life—the back-to-basics simplicity of living on a boat, the relaxed pace, the casual style, the comfort and independence of traveling in our own home, the freedom to come and go as we pleased, and the fascinating succession of people we met, both natives and other yachties.

CRUISING AND THE SEARCH
FOR UTOPIA

CRUISING IS A SLOW WAY to go. An island hop that takes 20 minutes by air can take eight hours under sail. An ocean crossed in eight hours by jet or five days by ship is a month's passage for a yacht. When the cruisers finally get to where they're going, they're likely to stay for a while.

Yachties have the luxury of time. Where other travelers dash in and out, yachties enjoy a leisurely pace. Our *Solanderi* was literally a slow boat to China; we spent a dozen years getting from the Virgin Islands to Hong Kong. En route we circled and crisscrossed the Caribbean, returning to Tortola several times, and made a couple of trips to the east coast of the United States and the Bahamas, then, after going through the Panama Canal, spent five years in the Pacific, cruising through the islands and living in Australia, New Zealand and Guam.

With our stop-and-go lifestyle, we could "do" a country in depth. If we liked it we stayed, for as long as it felt right. Peter got jobs. We both worked on the boat. We lived more or less as the locals did, except that our home was in the harbor rather than on a street. When we were ready to move on, we simply pulled up the anchor and sailed away.

Our wanderings were mostly among tropical islands. We liked the warm weather, and we liked the relaxed way of life. We never tired of the postcard-perfect scenery—the crescent shaped bays rimmed with white sand, palm trees swaying in the breeze, turquoise water shimmering in the sun. With the boat anchored in one of these idyllic coves, the highlight of each day was to swim in the translucent sea, then stretch out on deck and just gaze around at the beautiful view, while the water lapped rhythmically against the side and gently rocked the boat. We wondered what the poor people were doing, the ones who were so busy making money they didn't have time to "smell the flowers." We were privileged, and we appreciated it.

Each island is different, and we never knew exactly what to expect at the next one. Would it be mountainous and lush or flat and dry? Are the people black, brown or tan? Are they long and lean or short and stocky? Handsome or ugly? Friendly or reserved? Do they wear shorts or loincloths? Are their homes made of bamboo and grass or plywood and tin? Do they fish, garden, make canoes, weave mats, carve wood?

We stopped at scores of islands. Our curiosity about them was so insatiable we rarely passed one by, for fear of missing something good.

Did we find Utopia? Yes and no. When pressed to name my favorite place, my mind jumps to the South Pacific, but it doesn't stay in any one spot. It lingers longest in the Society Islands of French Polynesia, remembering the beauty of Moorea, the dancing in Bora

Bora and an anchorage in Huahine. To complete my perfect South Sea country, I'll add the people of Fiji, the houses of Samoa and the crafts of Tonga.

Most islands are beautiful but Moorea, the sister island of Tahiti, is the one that made me say aaah, here we are in Paradise at last. It was visually perfect, with spectacular mountains, lovely green hills, two big beautiful bays, dazzling beaches, a fabulous barrier reef completely surrounding the island and a gorgeous lagoon inside.

Even the homes and gardens of Moorea were consistently pretty. I hope that hordes of tourists haven't made it less attractive; daily ferry service from Tahiti was initiated shortly after our visit.

My perfect anchorage was on Moorea's neighbor, Huahine, in the middle of a sleepy lagoon, the reef a mile away, the island a mile the other way, not another boat or person in sight, the water brilliant turquoise, absolutely calm and so clear that from the deck we could see the shells on the white sandy bottom. I felt the boat was absolutely safe, and I wanted to swim forever.

The people throughout the Pacific were wonderfully friendly and hospitable, but the natives of Fiji populate my ideal island because we felt most comfortable with them. Melanesians with quite a lot of Polynesian mixed in, they are dark brown, tall and slim.

Both men and women wear short "Afro" hair styles, as they have for centuries, and dress in traditional *sulus*, or sarongs. The men wear shirts with their skirt-length *sulus*, and the women wear tunics with floor-length sarongs, a dignified and regal-looking style.

When we were there the Fijian culture was still based primarily on tribal traditions, yet the country was quite progressive. Even on remote outer islands everyone seemed to be quite well-educated. Although Fiji had been independent for years English was still taught in the schools, and we enjoyed intelligent conversations with people whose manners were much like our own.

Outside of the cities, most of the houses or huts in the Pacific islands are made of natural materials. The "little grass shacks" are put together from whatever is available locally—reeds, bamboo, pandanus leaves, palm tree trunks and fronds. Each island group has its own individual style, and they're all delightfully picturesque, but the houses in my Utopia are the *fales* (pronounced follies) of Samoa, which have no walls. The roof, which can be round, oval or rectangular, is supported by posts. If privacy or protection from the weather is required straw mats are rolled down like window shades. There is little or no furniture; more straw mats are rolled open and spread on the dirt floor when someone wants to sit or lie down.

Hands are busy throughout the Pacific creating a variety of attractive things, but the Tongans made our favorite crafts. My perfect island is decorated with their handsome straw baskets, mats and trays; amusing wood carvings; and the *tapa* cloths they pound out of mulberry tree bark, cover with powerful geometric designs and color with vibrant natural dyes.

No island in the South Pacific is complete without its custom dancing, but what a difference between the cultures! The farther west we went, the more sedate the dancing became, until finally the "dancers" were sitting down and the only movement was in their arms and heads! We much preferred the excited, erotic, foot-stomping, hip-shimmying style of the French islands' *tamure*, a charged-up relative of the languid Hawaiian hula.

We were lucky enough to be in Bora Bora for the week-long celebration of Bastille Day and to see numerous troupes of *tamure* dancers perform in a week-long contest. The brown-skinned, black-haired women in their grass skirts, coconut-shell bras and elaborate headdresses epitomize the romance of the South Sea islands and are a "must" ingredient of my perfect place.

YACHTIES

CRUISING YACHTIES come from all over the world and they sail in all directions. They are all ages (including octogenarians), from all kinds of backgrounds and of every personality type.

They sail alone, with entire families, with friends or with crew, but mostly with just a mate—a spouse or special friend. The cruising population has its share of long happy marriages, but the mating game is active and, because of the itinerant lifestyle, couples are often quite mixed. A New Zealand yachtie picks up a girlfriend in South Africa, a Canadian acquires a wife in Tonga, an Englishman loses his British wife in Italy but gains an American companion in Israel, who sails with him as far as the Caribbean, where she leaves him for a Dutchman. And so on.

Cruising companions must be quite compatible to handle the extraordinary demands on their relationships, especially at sea, where the solitude and loneliness of the setting are juxtaposed with the enforced togetherness of the crew. Even in port, most yachtie couples are alone together much of the time, quite dependent on each other for most of their physical, emotional, social and psychological needs. I considered myself extremely lucky to have Peter as my constant companion. He was such good company I never felt lonely for other friends or family but, thanks to Peter's more outgoing personality, we did get to know a lot of the other people who had chosen our alternative lifestyle.

Yachties are a vital group. The outdoor life gives them a healthy glow, and they are necessarily physically fit. Life aboard a cruising yacht is a continual workout—climbing ladders, rowing dinghies, raising sails, pulling up anchors and chains. Push-button mechanisms do exist on some boats, but yachties are characteristically active and strong. Most of the men I knew were, like Peter, attractively wiry.

The women were usually in good shape, too, although cruising tasks were often divided along traditional sexist lines. Typically, the men handled most of the physically demanding work on deck while the women were in charge of the cooking and other domestic chores. Very few of us "first mates" desired equal rights; a lot of us were in the cruising scene not for the love of sailing but for the love of a man who happened to love to sail.

The cruising fraternity was open and friendly and life in port was often quite sociable. Yachties visited back and forth, drinking endless cups of coffee and tea while swapping books, charts, information about anchorages and ports, practical advice and sea stories. The men almost always slid into a technical discussion and, while they were talking nuts and bolts, the women usually traded recipes.

If there were several boats in an anchorage, there was likely to be a party, often a bring-your-own cookout on a beach or pot luck at a yacht club ashore.

Yachties traditionally like their booze, and if there was a cheap bar ashore, cruisers were likely to meet there in the evenings. If not, there was often a gathering on one of the boats. Since *Solanderi* was usually the biggest boat around, she was often the site of an impromptu party. One thing I learned as hostess was: *Yachties never go home until you feed them.* Too many times, after hours of drinking and nibbling, when all I wanted to do was sleep, I realized I had to produce a real meal if we were ever to get rid of our laid-back visitors. Annoyed and tipsy, I reluctantly threw together a lot of spaghetti dinners just so that I could get to bed.

In this socially casual world, we knew each other by first names only. There were some yachties we met over and over again, in different ports around the world, whom we considered quite good friends, but often it wasn't unless we exchanged permanent addresses that we learned their surnames—and, sometimes, discovered whether a couple was married or not.

Conversation was rarely personal. Where you came from or what you had done in the "real" world were not often topics of discussion, not necessarily because the yachties had anything to hide or because they were running away from their past. Those subjects simply had nothing to do with cruising, and yachties rarely talked about anything else.

Cruising yachties are by definition always going somewhere else, but the pace varies. Some are in perpetual motion, like the middle-aged couple we met in Pago Pago who were on their fifth circumnavigation of the world. Others are prone to what we called "harbor rot"; they keep finding excuses to stay in one place. In between are the majority who cruise in spurts; for several months they are on the move, then they stop somewhere for months or years, usually to make some money or to work on the boat.

There are cruisers who set out with a specific plan and actually stick to it; they sail around the world in exactly the three years allotted to their adventure and then go home again. But most of the yachties we met got side-tracked somewhere along the way and one of the things they grew to cherish was the freedom to postpone, revise or simply cancel the current plan. Schedules, itineraries and destinations became less important as the cruisers became more relaxed, and finally "getting there" became a goal in itself. When I met Peter he was on his way to the Pacific, but it was seven years before he finally reached it. "I don't want to rush it," he often said. "I might not pass this way again."

THE YACHTIE STYLE

MOST YACHTIES ARE READILY recognized by their natural look and casual-to-grubby attire. Their skin is sun-tanned and weather-beaten, their hair is wind-blown and sun-bleached, their clothes are faded and worn, and sometimes dirty and torn.

The laid-back yachtie style is partly conscious choice, partly dictated by the exposed environment of boats, where a constant barrage of wind, sun and salt water make grooming attempts a waste of time. No matter how neat a yachtie starts out, he's likely to look quite unkempt by the time he gets to shore.

Like many cruising couples, Peter and I cut each other's hair, a custom that contributed significantly to our scruffy appearance. I occasionally had a professional cut when we reached a civilized port but Peter wouldn't spend the money, even though all I could do with his floppy hair was make it look like a thatched roof. He teased that I did it deliberately, to keep the other girls away. I also clipped his beard which was full and curly but kept fairly short.

Most of the men in the cruising world have beards. They are an important ingredient of the seafaring image but they are practical too. A beard protects the face from the elements (I often wished I had one) and it eliminates the dangerous practice of shaving on a bouncing boat.

Cruising wardrobes on most yachts are limited by storage space. The few clothes yachties have are casual and comfortable, wrinkled and abused. They are stored in small, cramped lockers and never pressed because most yachts have only 12-volt electric systems that can't handle irons. They are washed in a bucket, dried by the wind and constantly exposed to sun, salt, dampness, mildew and rust. And, because most yachties are always working on their boats, the clothes are also likely to be spotted with paint, varnish, grease and/or glue, so that even when just scrubbed, they look dirty. In yachtie wardrobes, it's often a toss-up whether a particular garment belongs on the body or in the rag bag.

Foul weather gear, which the British call oilskins or oilies, is a must for every yachtie, a waterproof outfit to keep out rain and sea spray—a jacket with hood, pants and boots. Warm sweaters and socks are also needed, even in the tropics, because once a sailor is wet he's also cold.

When the weather is warm yachties wear as little as possible onboard—bikinis, shorts, sarongs or nothing at all.

The standard going-ashore outfit is a T-shirt and shorts, with flip-flops, if anything, on the feet. When it's cool or buggy, yachties wear sweatshirts and jeans.

I always had at least one skirt aboard for going ashore, because in the less developed countries, the inhabitants are often shocked and offended to see a bit of female thigh. On some of the Pacific islands the women go topless, but their upper legs are always covered, even when they're bathing in the sea.

Yachties of both sexes have adopted the sarong of the Pacific islanders as a favorite article of clothing. It is simply a rectangle of cotton cloth wrapped around the body and tied in a knot above the bust or on the hips. It's cool, comfortable and quick and easy to put on and take off. *Lava-lava* is the Polynesian word for a sarong. In French its *pareu*, in Papua New Guinea *lap-lap*, in Fiji *sulu*. The material is usually a bright, bold floral print, but some are elaborate batiks.

Yachties copy islanders in their footgear as well. Some of them do wear those expensive leather shoes made for boating, but we went barefoot on the boat and wore Japanese rubber sandals ashore. They are perfect for cruisers because they're cheap, readily available and waterproof. The islanders leave them outside the door when they enter a house; yachties leave them in the dinghy when they get back on the boat. We called these shoes flip-flops but again we heard many variations—go-aheads and zories, thongs in Australia and jandals in New Zealand.

As prime candidates for skin cancer, most yachties try to cover their heads, but it's hard to keep a hat on your head in a good sailing breeze. The obvious solution is to tie it under the chin, but that's uncomfortable. Peter and I wore shirts with collars and buttonholes when the sun was strong, so we simply attached a hat to a buttonhole with a string. The wind could still whip the hat off the head, but at least it wasn't lost over the side.

My fashion standards changed radically after I moved onto the boat. As a professional woman working in New York and San Juan I had shopped in department stores and boutiques, kept up with the latest styles and had a closet full of good clothes and shoes, Puccis and Guccis included.

When I moved aboard *Solanderi* almost everything had to go, and I never missed my city wardrobe. I loved the casual barefoot life, and in no time I looked as scruffy as Peter did. I was allotted a small locker for my clothes, about two cubic feet, and into it went all my underwear, bathing suits, shorts, shirts, sarongs, jeans and sweat shirts. There was no way to expand the storage area, so if I acquired a new shirt I had to get rid of an old one.

As my good clothes wore out, I replaced them with cheaper and cheaper things. In the end I was as avid a bargain hunter as Peter, and thrift shops were my favorite haunts.

JOBS

IF THERE WERE ANY RICH yachties I didn't know them. We did meet a few people who were able to cruise for several years without working but most of them had to augment their income eventually if they wanted to keep on cruising. Others, like Peter, set sail with empty pockets, prepared from the beginning to work their way from port to port.

Yachties aren't proud. The jobs they take to keep from starving or to replenish the kitty are often menial and underpaid. As transient and often illegal workers, they don't have a lot of choice.

Most of the men are, like Peter, jacks of all trades. They get temporary jobs as mechanics, welders, fiberglassers, machinists, carpenters, painters and varnishers.

18

The women work as cooks, bar maids, waitresses, chambermaids, baby sitters, seamstresses, painters and varnishers.

Few yachties found jobs in the trade or profession for which they were trained; it wasn't unusual to find a school teacher serving beer or an electronics technician pumping gas. But we did know of some notable exceptions, like the dentist who practiced on board with a reclining chair under a skylight in his salon, a seamstress who made huge awnings in the tiny cabin of her yacht, pilots who flew 10 days a month and sailed 20, and a ship's officer who sped across oceans in a freighter once or twice a year, then returned to his yacht to continue his own slow progress around the world.

Most yachties liked to work close to home (Peter's idea of a good job was one within rowing distance), but we knew some who secured their boats in safe harbors or boatyards for a few months while they went inland to work at ski resorts or cattle ranches. A few who were really anxious about their finances left the boat for a year or more "on the hard" while they flew back to the States or some other homeland to pick up their careers and replenish their bank accounts.

Artists and writers who could work on board were envied and were never out of work. We met several yachties who did quite well painting watercolors, carving scrimshaw or writing up their adventures for various publications.

Yachties accomplished in a craft could sometimes make ends meet by making things like jewelry, tooled leather bags or crocheted bikinis to peddle to other yachties and shops ashore. One friend sold bikinis as fast as she could make them by dinghying around to other yachts in the harbor clad only in one of her samples.

Some boat owners with an entrepreneurial spirit avoided taking jobs by taking on paying crew. There were always budget-minded but adventurous travelers delighted to pay a reasonable fare for the opportunity to sail. Most of them considered it a privilege to haul the anchor and stand the midnight watch as well.

19

Peter was usually hungry enough to do any job that came along. His formal training was as a machinist (called fitter-turner in England where he did his apprenticeship). He practiced his trade for about one year in his teens, before he discovered yachting. From then on it was any job he could get as he worked his way from port to port, living virtually hand to mouth.

He worked as a welder, machinist, sand blaster, carpenter, fiberglasser and auto mechanic, but he was happiest working on boats. When I first knew him he was enjoying life as a free-lance skipper for the charter yachts in Tortola. Getting paid to go sailing and eat steaks was his idea of the good life.

In between charters and our own cruising, he also did a lot of general handyman work on the yachts and eventually was offered a steady job as maintenance supervisor for one of the charter fleets. That meant real money for a change, but what an agonizing decision because a condition of the job was that he agree to take it for at least a year. Peter couldn't imagine staying in one place for such a long time. But he finally accepted it and even did a second year's stint so that by the time we left for the Pacific he actually had some money in the bank.

Later he found his true calling as a delivery captain. When a yacht needs to get from one place to another and the owner doesn't have the time or interest to make the trip, he hires a captain to deliver it for him. It's usually a long passage and likely to be an unpleasant one—into the wind, out of the tropical latitudes and/or non-stop. But for Peter, being paid a few thousand dollars for a few weeks of sailing, no matter how hard, was a terrific deal. A long delivery, from the Marshall Islands to San Francisco, or from the Philippines to Samoa, financed his cruising for another year.

I was one of the lucky ones who didn't have to work. I certainly wasn't rich, but I had a few dividends coming in and, thanks to our very modest style of living, little going out. Peter was reluctant to accept money from me but, considering his circumstances, it seemed ridiculous for me not to pay my own way. Besides, I saw no reason to eat rice and beans every day if I didn't have to. Eventually we worked out an arrangement that kept us both happy. We each paid for our own personal expenses—clothes, dentists, air fares, *etc.*, I paid for the groceries and he bought everything for the boat.

It was lucky for *Solanderi* that I didn't have to work for money. It meant that whenever we stopped cruising for a while I could stay home and work on the boat, for love. That is when we caught up on routine maintenance. While Peter was working somewhere else or away on a delivery, I spent all day sanding, painting and varnishing— tedious, backbreaking work, but still preferable to anything I might have done ashore. I had only to think about a friend in New Zealand who cleaned hotel rooms in the morning and fried fish and chips in the afternoon to be forever grateful for my financial independence.

21

CRUISING YACHTS
AND THE MONOHULL VS.
MULTIHULL DEBATE

THE YACHTS THAT CRISSCROSS the oceans of the world are old and new, elegant and ugly, mass-produced and homemade. They are almost exclusively sailboats because motor boats are too dependent on fuel sources to be viable for long-distance cruising.

They are big and small but mostly between 30 and 40 feet, large enough to live aboard with some comfort but manageable for one or two people.

They are made of wood, fiberglass, ferro-cement, steel or, occasionally, aluminum.

There are monohulls and multihulls. There are sloops, cutters, ketches, yawls, schooners and junks, each identified by the number, size and placement of its masts.

The floating homes of cruising yachties are so diverse and usually so individualized it's almost safe to say there are no two alike.

The only thing all cruising yachts have in common is that they are loaded down with gear. Unlike streamlined racing yachts and tidy weekend sailboats, the cruising yacht carries all the equipment necessary for sailing in the open sea plus food and supplies to sustain its occupants for months or even years. Cruising yachts sit much lower in the water than their empty counterparts.

They are easily recognized. The rigging bristles with satellite navigation devices, radar and radar reflectors, radio antennae and poles for supporting sails. Weird contraptions to steer the boat sprout from the stern. The decks and cabin tops are covered with dinghies, life rafts, containers of water and fuel, diving equipment, propane bottles, anchors, chains, ropes and bags full of sails. And on most cruising yachts these days there is at least one large oval board lashed to the lifelines, because wind surfing—or board sailing—is what yachties do for recreation when they are in port.

Each of the yacht types has its ardent champions. As crew on a catamaran, I was naturally most familiar with the arguments concerning the relative merits of two hulls as opposed to one or three.

Thanks to Dennis Conner's racing *Stars and Stripes* in the America's Cup, everyone knows now that a catamaran is a two-hull boat of shallow draft and light construction that is *fast*!

Multihulls, a term encompassing both catamarans and trimarans, which have three hulls, were developed for their speed. They skim along with just a foot or two under the surface of the water, often sailing circles around monohulls, which are dragging a keel full of lead through six or so feet of sea.

Their appeal as racing yachts is obvious but, of course, when modified for cruising and loaded down with all the owners' worldly possessions, a "multi" sacrifices much of its speed. Certainly *Solanderi* had nothing more in common with *Stars and Stripes* than a recreational vehicle has with a racing car.

But speed is only one of the areas of debate between the traditional "monos" and the relatively new and different "cats" and "tris."

Many traditionalists dismiss multihulls as unsafe because they can capsize. Multi enthusiasts counter with yes, but they don't sink. The lead keel that keeps a mono from rolling all the way over can also drag it to the bottom when the boat is full of water, whereas the buoyant construction materials and watertight bulkheads of most multis keep them afloat even when there's a hole in the bottom.

It's alarmingly easy for a yacht to be holed—by another vessel, a rock or reef, flotsam or jetsam (including steel containers that fall off cargo ships and float almost completely submerged), a whale or other large fish or even by its own mast or boom if it breaks away from the rigging.

I was reassured to think that, despite such a catastrophe, our catamaran could continue to float. Our hulls were made of plywood and fiberglass, and we had two watertight bulkheads in each hull. Theoretically, any flooding would be contained in the damaged compartment. The boat might become an ungainly raft, but that was certainly preferable to no boat at all.

If a multihull capsizes, it becomes an upside-down raft. Many multi builders put a hatch in the bottom of each hull so that if the boat does turn over while they're inside it, they simply have to open the hatch and climb out. Peter considered that an unnecessary precaution, and felt the same way about a ball on top of the mast, a device which is supposed to thwart a capsize when the mast meets the water.

His theory was that multihulls "turn turtle" only if they are over-canvassed, that is, carrying too much sail for the weather conditions, as often happens in a race. He was convinced that with proper handling, his cat would never capsize, and it never did.

However, just in case, we always painted the bottom a high visibility red or international orange.

Draft, the depth of water necessary for a boat to float, is another hot subject of debate.

The shallow draft of multihulls is what attracts many owners. A cat or tri that draws only a couple of feet of water can go almost anywhere—into shallow channels, over sandbars and coral heads, close to shore, even on the beach. To monohullers, such versatility is not as important as the "performance" they achieve with their keels. A weighted boat is much more responsive to the helm than a multi, turning easily and "pointing" well. Multis like *Solanderi* maneuver about as spryly as a tanker.

The quality of motion is another argument for and against the number of hulls. Monohulls pitch and yaw and rock and roll, but it's a smoother, steadier ride than on catamarans, which pitch and yaw and jerk, bounce, lurch and hobby-horse. However, I for one could handle all those motions better than the rolling of a monohull.

I also liked the relative spaciousness of the cat and I loved being upright. We called monos "leaners," because when they're not rolling they're usually heeled over on one side. Sailing at this unnatural and uncomfortable angle, the cook is strapped to the stove, the sleeper is boarded into his bunk, and anyone who wants to move around has to use hands and feet in a feat Peter called "walking on the walls."

Even eating is a contest against gravity. Plates for yachts are a lot like those for babies with high sides and sections to keep the foods from running together and suction rings to keep the plates on the table. Yet food can still slide off. One mono owner we knew got so tired of losing his dinner he resorted to eating out of dog bowls instead.

There was plenty of good-natured rivalry between mono and multi enthusiasts in the cruising fraternity, but we didn't encounter any actual snobbery. In some yacht club and racing circles I understand that traditionalists really look down their noses at multihulls, especially the homemade variety like Peter's, but in all our travels we never felt discriminated against. In the cruising world it seemed that any vessel was okay as long as it was capable of getting its owner to wherever he wanted to go.

I was never aware of any particular qualities that differentiated multihull sailors from others but, on the basis of the names they chose for their boats, I'll venture to say they took themselves a little less seriously than single-hull sailors.

We saw trimarans named *Do-Re-Mi*, and *Try Me* and catamarans called *Wise Cat* and *Null and Void*. If Peter had named his boat I'm sure he too would have made a pun.

Monohull cruisers tended to be much more serious, even poetic, when naming their yachts. There was *Sea Swan* and *Wind Song*, *Moonracer* and *Stargazer*, *Aquarius* and *Sirius*, *Born Free* and *Liberty*, *Vagabond* and *Wanderer*, even *White Squall* and *Stormy Weather*.

Ships and boats are traditionally named after women but, strangely enough, I saw only a handful of cruising yachts with female names.

Solanderi was named after a fish. The couple that built the boat wanted to call her *Wahoo*, a lively name for a fast and pretty fish, but it was already taken; in British registry, only one vessel to a name is allowed. Disappointed, they settled for *Solanderi*, the ponderous name of the species.

We got tired of having to explain what it meant, but Peter never considered changing it, because in nautical tradition that's bad luck, and most sailors are notoriously superstitious.

HOME AFLOAT

SOLANDERI WAS A 45-FOOT CATAMARAN designed by James Wharram. Wharram cats are popular do-it-yourself boats, being easier, quicker and cheaper to make than most others. Basically, they have two plywood canoe-shaped hulls sheathed in fiberglass and joined by four crossbeams, some decking and nets. They look like grown-up versions of the fast, tippy Hobie cats that race off every shore.

Wharram designs, which come in several sizes, are based on the Polynesian "double canoes" that have sailed the Pacific Ocean for centuries. Wharram added a revolutionary element, rubber mounts between the beams and decks, so that the boat is flexible instead of rigid and all the parts "work" independently of each other.

Wharram, a Welshman renowned for cruising with a crew of naked women, is dismissed as a crazy eccentric by some traditionalists, but his distinctive yachts sail all over the world. They don't win prizes for speed or performance or beauty, but they are affordable, seaworthy do-it-yourself boats.

Those who build Wharrams tend to be as individualistic as the man who designed them. We never met one who followed the plans exactly. Some stretched the length, others modified the rigging and almost everyone beefed up the beams. A few departed radically from the original concept with some highly unconventional variations.

In New Zealand we met a farmer/sailor who raised pigs on an offshore island and sailed them to market on the mainland in his Wharram cat. The stern section of his deck was hinged so that it could drop down like a ramp. He backed up to a beach, loaded his pigs aboard, raised the ramp and set sail for Auckland.

In Australia we saw a Wharram used as a platform for a huge houseboat. A two-story "cabin," complete with household furniture and appliances, was built on deck. A mast protruded from the top and the "boat" was rigged for sailing, as if that ungainly mass was really expected to move.

Many Wharrams are built on the cheap but I wonder if one we encountered in an Australian river ever floated. A Yugoslavian oboe player was building his hulls out of packing cases and he planned to use two inverted lifeboats as detachable cabin tops.

Compared to these extremes, Peter's Wharram cat looked quite traditional and yachty.

Although Peter didn't make *Solanderi*, he rebuilt her extensively over the years, changing the rig, adding to the width and enlarging the cabins. He made so many changes the original owners recognized her only by her distinctive color scheme when we met them in New Caledonia.

Solanderi had powder blue hulls, royal blue bulwarks, beige decks and white trim.

When I moved aboard, she was a very basic yacht. There was no electricity and no refrigeration. There was a head (toilet), but it was reached through an opening in the deck; if the hatch was closed for privacy or to keep out rain or spray, it was impossible to see—or breathe for very long.

Our greatest deficiency in my opinion was a proper engine. Most cruising sailboats rely quite heavily on their auxiliary power. *Solanderi*, an unwieldy catamaran, had only a seven-horsepower outboard motor to help her in tight spots. That motor was more appropriate for a large dinghy.

Over the years we acquired what Peter considered a few luxuries, including fluorescent lights all over the boat, a small gas refrigerator, a proper head and two 15-horsepower diesel engines.

The living accommodations on a Wharram cat are squeezed into the two narrow hulls. On the port or left side was our galley (kitchen) and salon (or saloon, as the sitting/dining area is called on British yachts). Ours was simply a large table and an L-shaped bench. The starboard or right hull had two bunks and the head and dressing area. The "master bunk" was slightly larger than a single bed but we could sleep in it together as long as we both kept slim.

In port we lived and slept on deck. An area between the hulls, about 10 feet square (spacious by yacht standards), was our breezy living/dining/bedroom with an unobstructed 360-degree view. A large awning protected us from the sun and rain and a spray dodger could be raised if it was too windy. We gradually turned the area into quite a comfortable, good-looking home, with two built-in "settees," lots of colorful pillows, a folding table and a straw mat on the "floor." At night we moved the cushions from the settees to the center deck and that was our double bed.

All the furnishings were stowed below when we went sailing but as soon as the anchor was down again, up would go our instant house.

The overall deck space on *Solanderi* was so big our visitors likened it to a tennis court or ballroom and, in fact, during our years in Tortola, when we did a lot of partying and discotecs were all the rage, we actually did dance on deck, calling the boat the Discodeck and what we did on it the Decodance.

ENGINES

MOST CRUISING SAILBOATS have some kind of engine. Although the wind in the sails is the principal means of locomotion, there are times when the wind doesn't blow and there are circumstances in which even a supremely confident captain feels the need for auxiliary power, such as when entering a crowded harbor.

Monohulls typically have a diesel engine of about 15 horsepower nestled in the hull. Catamarans and trimarans, which have shallow hulls and are more weight conscious, are more likely to have outboard motors.

Since few yachts seem to enjoy the luxury of a trouble-free engine, most yachties are forced to learn something about motor mechanics. They develop a love-hate relationship with the demanding engines they are so dependent upon and often christen them in anger. My favorite was a really problematic German engine named "Hitler" by its enraged owner.

Solanderi started out with a vintage 7-horsepower Chrysler outboard motor, far from adequate for a 45-foot catamaran, but Peter cheerfully made the best of what he had. *Solanderi* was an unresponsive yacht, difficult to maneuver under sail or power. We needed a wide open space to turn around. With just a little outboard to propel us, our passage through an anchorage was quite eventful. Somehow Peter managed to avoid any disastrous collisions but his jousting and feinting at other boats in a harbor made me a nervous wreck.

Our next step up from the Chrysler was a "Peter Special," a 50-horsepower outboard motor in the Rube Goldberg tradition. My inventive captain put together parts from two engines of different makes—a Mercury top salvaged from the bottom of the sea and a Johnson bottom found in a junkyard. To these he added an elongated three-foot stainless steel shaft which he made himself, without benefit of machine tools, in a workshop in Tortola where he was doing odd jobs.

It worked! It was certainly an improvement over the Chrysler. Now we needed only half a harbor to turn around in. "The Mixmaster," also known as "The Monster" on bad days, needed constant attention, which Peter faithfully gave it for the next 10 years. It got us all over the Caribbean and the Pacific and, just barely, through the Panama Canal.

Most yachts transit the canal tied up to a larger vessel but, because of our fragile plywood bulwarks, Peter elected to go "center lock," meaning we were alone in the middle of the canal with four long lines to the shore, two on each side, held by four men who walked us forward as each lock filled and we moved on to the next.

We had been warned to expect a fierce current when the gates of the last lock opened. Peter had the engine running full speed but still the current got us and *Solanderi* swung broadside. Our line holders had to let go. The pilot assigned to shepherd us through the canal hid his head in his hands. It was up to Peter to straighten us out. He gunned the engine backward and forward, coming within inches of the wall on each pass before throwing it into the opposite gear.

He finally got us headed straight for the open gate and we shot out of the lock and shakily retrieved our lines. Four 120-foot lines had been wildly swirling around in the water, but it was our lucky day; none of them fouled the prop or the rudders.

The Monster was a noisy, smelly gas guzzler which was mainly used to get us in and out of harbors and other tight spots. We did try motoring up the intracoastal waterway on the east coast of the U.S. and the Rio Dulce in Guatemala, but they weren't very pleasant trips.

When we were in Australia and planning to cruise around the equator where the winds are very light, Peter started shopping around for a second-hand inboard diesel engine. I was so thrilled at the idea of having real power I offered to pay for a new one.

We ended up ordering *two* diesel engines from Japan. From the ridiculous to the sublime! Peter worked it out that we could get two small ones for the price of one large one if we could avoid the steep Australian import tax. For his two-hulled yacht one small engine on each side was ideal, far better than one large one in the middle or on one side. So we had the engines sent to our next port of call, Noumea in New Caledonia, where he installed one 15-horsepower Yanmar in each hull.

What luxury! Then we could motor for hours at a time if we wanted to. And ponderous old *Solanderi* could turn on a dime. I loved the maneuverability and the ease of anchoring without the fear of wiping out another boat.

We named our darling engines "Ichiban" (number one in Japanese) and "Ichitwo."

MAINTENANCE

WHAT DO YACHTIES DO when they're not at sea? They work on the boat, that's what. There's a well-known adage in nautical circles: A boat is a hole in the water into which you pour money. For do-it-yourself yachties, a boat is a hole in the water into which you pour money, time and energy.

Wood and steel boats require more maintenance than fiberglass or ferro-cement, but I never met a person on any kind of cruising yacht who ran out of things to do.

There is the constant routine maintenance of painting and varnishing, tinkering with the engine and tuning the wires (also known as frigging with the rigging). And then there is The List. On most cruising yachts there are so many things breaking down and wearing out, it's exhausting just to look at the list of jobs to do after each passage: mend the mainsail, fix the salt water pump, adjust the compass, splice the anchor line, move a cleat, re-caulk a deck seam, *etc., etc.*—and that's on a basically simple yacht like Peter's. I hate to think of the lists on the yachts full of electric and electronic gear.

Peter was a believer in the KISS principle (Keep It Simple, Stupid) on the theory that the more things he had, the more he'd have to fix. Over the years he succumbed to a few luxuries but ours was still one of the simpler cruising yachts.

Nevertheless, *Solanderi* kept both of us so busy I frequently complained in my diary that we didn't have time for any fun.

Peter's life centered around his boat and he couldn't stop working on it. If he wasn't doing routine maintenance or crossing jobs off The List, he was usually tearing the boat apart and rebuilding it bigger and better.

Major surgery was scheduled almost every year when we stopped cruising for the hurricane season. He replaced the clunky rudders with more streamlined, efficient ones. He built a new set of crossbeams at least twice, making them bigger and stronger each time. He replaced the rotting bulwarks in a surprisingly difficult job that dragged on so long we called it The Year of the Bulwarks. And he enlarged the living accommodations often, raising a roof here, pushing out a cabin side there, then a few years later doing it all over again to gain another few inches of comfort.

The deck was his workshop and there was always something strewn across it—engine parts or plywood and sawdust or fiberglass and resin or sailcloth and the sewing machine. His materials cost as little as possible. Half of the storage areas on the boat were stuffed with things that might come in handy—scraps of metal, wood and plastic; bits of wire and rope; tins full of nails and screws and nuts and bolts in every size and description. The stuff that man carried around! I called the boat a floating junkyard but I was grateful that he was good about stowing the junk out of sight when he wasn't working with it.

If he didn't have what he needed for the current job in his own lockers, Peter checked with the other yachts, the garbage dumps and the junkyards. Only if he couldn't get something for nothing did he start shopping around. Marine stores were entered only as a last resort. He called them jewelry stores because of their high prices.

Anything labeled "for marine use" has a tremendous markup. Yachting is, after all, the sport of kings. But Peter was not one to be reached by snob appeal; he was much more comfortable rummaging through the dusty merchandise in a Chinese general store or patronizing a no-nonsense hardware store. He even gave up buying marine paint when he found that household varieties seemed to hold up just as well and cost about half as much.

That was an important discovery for us, as we used a lot of paint. With two 45-foot hulls and a 20-foot-wide deck, we seemed to have acres of surface to protect. I was in charge of the "cosmetics" (paint and varnish) and I worked on them full-time whenever Peter wasn't working on the boat. I developed tennis elbow in both arms when I was on *Solanderi*, and I blame the hours of sanding and painting for the condition.

Thanks to Peter's KISS principle we had no varnish on deck except for the wheel. Varnished trim is attractive and traditional on yachts but requires even more upkeep than paint, especially when exposed continually to the tropical sun. Peter was afraid that if he had to keep up varnish he'd never have time to go sailing.

Painting the bottom of the boat is a necessary chore that recurs about annually. The part of the boat that's in the water all the time has a magnetic attraction for a variety of sea life, from small animals to large plants. Bottom paint, or anti-fouling, resists that attraction, but not for long. After about six months a slime starts to adhere, then the critters return and before long an underwater garden is in full bloom again. The growth can be scrubbed off a few times while the boat is in the water, but eventually the bottom must be painted again.

One of the greatest attractions of multihulls is that they can be beached for bottom painting, saving the expense and inconvenience of a boatyard "haul out."

With *Solanderi* we positioned the boat at high tide and, as the water dropped, ran around with scrapers and sandpaper getting off all the growth and old paint. Then, because we were usually in places with very small tides, it was a race against time to get on two coats of paint before the tide returned to the waterline and the boat floated.

We were eaten by mosquitoes, bitten by crabs and sucked into mud, and sometimes we worked by the light of the moon, but we saved about a thousand dollars a year with our do-it-yourself haulouts.

We did all our own sewing as well: sails, awnings, cushion covers and the blankety-blank dodger, all big and bulky, all heavy-duty jobs, and all repetitive. Thanks to the tropical sun, everything had to be replaced every few years.

Peter was good at it, having learned sewing skills from his mother, a professional seamstress. He never attempted to make a sail from scratch but he remade plenty of hand-me-downs and we were forever repairing sails: resewing seams and reinforcing corners and patching holes.

When I first knew him, Peter was sewing everything by hand. He looked like a character in a Conrad saga, sitting on deck hunched over a voluminous sail, patiently remaking it, stitch by stitch.

When he learned that second-hand industrial sewing machines were plentiful and cheap in Puerto Rico, he splurged about $150 to buy one—without the motor, because he had nowhere to plug it in. He didn't anticipate that a few years later he would own a small generator, too.

Although we never knew for sure where the machine had come from, Peter enjoyed telling people it was from an old brassiere factory.

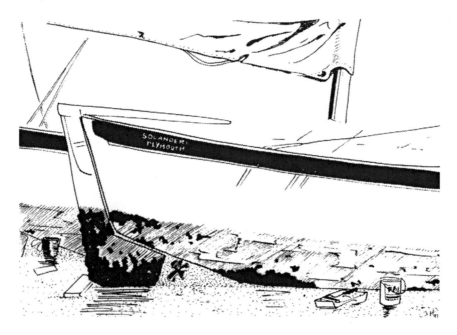

He always intended to make a treadle for it but he never did, so instead we cranked by hand. Most of the material we worked with was so large and awkward we had to work together. Peter turned the wheel and manhandled the sail or awning into the eight-inch hole; I used both hands to feed the material through.

With all the stop and go and push and pull involved in such a project, I was always quite bitchy by the end of a sewing session.

Even Peter lost his natural cheerfulness when it was time to make another spray dodger. A dodger keeps some of the sea spray out of the cockpit on a conventional boat. We used ours at anchor to keep driving rain and wind out of our home-on-deck. Like the top of a convertible car, a dodger is curved around metal pipes and can be raised or lowered to the deck as the weather dictates. There's something about their curvature that gives even professional sailmakers a hard time. It was one of the few things that brought out Peter's temper.

WHEELS

WHEN CRUISING YACHTIES go ashore they walk, hitchhike, ride buses and occasionally splurge on taxis. Some of them carry bikes on board. A few even have motorbikes. Only if they plan to stay in one place for a matter of months do they invest in a car and then, because it's just a temporary toy and because yachties focus all their money on their yachts, the car is likely to be just one step from the junkyard. As long as it gets them where they want to go, it doesn't matter what it looks like.

We had some real winners. Because Peter was fairly talented at keeping engines alive, we could have wheels of some description for a minimal investment and because Peter necessarily improved our cars, we usually got our money back when we moved on.

In New Zealand we bought an indigenous vehicle, a Trekka van. Even in a land where many people drive vintage cars and do-it-yourself is a way of life, our Trekka stood out in the crowd. Put together from three different mini-vans, it had a blue body, yellow hood and orange doors.

Peter fixed up the engine in the garage where he was working as a mechanic and, because we wanted to tour the country by car, he rigged up a plywood platform in the back where we could sleep—in a semi-fetal position. We painted the car all blue before we hit the road.

Our best bargain was a double header in Guam. In 1985 we acquired two Datsun rust buckets—a 1970 station wagon and a 1972 pickup—for $250. The truck, a derelict, was thrown in "for parts," just so that the owner could get the eyesore off his property. Was he surprised when a month later, after a couple of visits to the junkyard, Peter had the pickup on the road. With a homemade hood and tailgate, it even passed the motor vehicle inspection without a bribe.

Ours were typical "Guam Bombs." The station wagon was known as "the gas chamber" because of an inexhaustible cloud of foul smoke that came out of the tailpipe and back into the car. The pickup was, like our Trekka, a composite. The colors this time were faded maroon, green and black, and the entire body was lacy with rust.

Because the pickup was more reliable, and because my art class at the university was farther away than Peter's job at the machine shop, it was my vehicle, and although I'm not usually snobbish about what I drive, I have to admit I was embarrassed by that truck. I rarely reminisced about my distant past—the classy schools I had attended or the glossy magazines where I had worked—but driving that beat-up pickup made me image-conscious and I thought what a shock it would be to my former mentors if they could see me now!

Most of the time when we were cruising, Peter and I shared one bike. One small, Taiwan-made push bike that broke down into two

pieces, perfect for the boat because it was easy to get in and out of the dinghy and could be stowed in separate lockers below decks. I did a lot of grocery shopping on that bike, and Peter carried an amazing amount of hardware, lumber, paint and gas on the little thing. But we couldn't go anywhere together. I thought it would be nice to have two bikes.

We finally got a second one in Australia when Peter, a 40-year-old kid, made his own. New bikes were expensive and out of the question. Instead he found a bicycle repairman with a backyard full of used frames and a tumbledown shed full of parts, old and new. He bought all the pieces, spent a day putting them together and then, so that it could be stowed like the other one, sawed his new bicycle in half.

COOKING

NON-BOATERS AND WEEKEND sailors are usually impressed if they're offered anything more complicated than a peanut butter sandwich on a yacht. To them, eating on a boat means picnicking on snacks brought in a cooler from home.

And most sailboats are designed with that in mind. A tiny galley is squeezed into a corner of the main cabin, equipped with a small stove and sink and a large built-in icebox, the assumption being that a lot of cold drinks will be consumed but there won't be much preparation of food on board.

When such a boat becomes a home for "live aboards," the galley is as vitally important as any kitchen, as most yachties eat much the same as normal people do—three meals a day with a hot dinner at night.

Working with what amounts to basic camping gear, the cook must be quite creative to produce real meals and, yes, guests should be impressed by her accomplishments.

I refer to the cook as she because if there is a woman on board you can bet she's the one in the galley. In all my years of cruising I met only one couple that really worked at being "liberated." Each cooked alternate nights. Wonderful. *But* they also shared duties on deck. Not so wonderful on a dark and stormy night. I was happy to be the "galley slave" and leave the macho work to Peter.

Of course there are yachts equipped with all the household gadgets—refrigerators and freezers, food processors and microwaves. But they rarely venture far from marinas where they can plug in. They bear little resemblance to most of the sailboats on the cruising scene.

Electric appliances use far too much fuel for yachts without an umbilical cord to shore. Even the freezer-refrigerator units designed for cruising boats must be charged regularly for about an hour a day by the main engine or a generator. Most serious cruisers reject them because they don't want to be tied down to such a schedule, they don't like the noise and they don't want the expense.

Monohull cruisers have no alternative but to live without refrigeration. Their ice boxes might get filled on rare occasions, but the farther they go from civilization, the rarer and more expensive ice becomes. Yachties with stable multihulls, on the other hand, have an excellent option—camping fridges that run on propane gas or kerosene. Because the boats remain upright even at sea, the refrigerator never quits. We had a small one on *Solanderi* that operated all the time, even in the roughest weather. The same unit on a monohull would lose the pilot light as soon as the boat heeled.

Solanderi had a spacious galley by cruising yacht standards, about 10 feet long and four feet wide. We had an English-made propane stove (two burners, an oven and broiler), about the same size as the Dutch-made refrigerator (two cubic feet), a small sink and three feet of counter space, a positively luxurious feature. Many boats have absolutely no counters at all.

Stoves on cruising yachts run on propane gas, kerosene or, rarely, alcohol. They cover the gamut from four-burner household ranges to single hot plates. They don't necessarily reflect the abilities of the cook on board.

Some of the most impressive meals we ate were prepared on the most limited equipment. I think of a reunion we had in Sydney, Australia, with friends we had known in the Virgin Islands. Their yacht had a two-burner counter-top kerosene stove. The meal she cooked to celebrate our visit included a "roast" (a leg of lamb seared in the frying pan and "roasted" in the pressure cooker) and a deliciously light and airy cake "baked" in a metal contraption over a burner, her stove-top "oven."

There is an amazingly large body of cookbooks supposedly written for cruisers, but they are apparently aimed at the weekend sailor who shops in a supermarket every Friday, certainly not at full-time wanderers like us. Rarely could I produce the package of frozen broccoli flowerettes or the four ounces of dairy sour cream their recipes called for.

Instead I considered it accomplishment enough if I could come up with a simple meal that was filling, nourishing and, hopefully, tasty. I never served more than one course and, whenever possible, used just one pot: a frying pan, wok, stew pot or pressure cooker.

Pressure cookers are considered essential on most cruising yachts for several reasons: They conserve on fuel, they make cheap cuts of meat edible, ditto conch and octopus, they can be used as ovens, they sterilize bacteria and they have locking lids that keep food in the pot when the sea is trying to toss it out.

We used a pressure cooker like a *pot au feu* but, instead of simmering on a back burner all day and night, our "stoup" was brought up to pressure every day and kept airtight. We called it stoup because sometimes it was thick like stew and sometimes thin like soup. I put all our leftovers in it—meat, vegetables, potatoes, rice, spaghetti and sauce, salad with dressing, even, after one memorable party, rum and coke and gin and tonic.

A four-month stoup went over the side when we flew from Antigua to England to visit Peter's family. Our boat-sitter, appalled to learn the contents of the pot, tossed it out the minute we left. She wouldn't even feed it to the dog!

Cooking in port may seem like an adventure to landlubbers, but it's tame stuff compared to cooking at sea. This is an occupation not to be contemplated by the faint-hearted. The boat is in constant motion, and so are the cook and the cooking pots.

On monohulls, when the boat is heeling, the cook is literally strapped to the stove to keep her from sliding away. On *Solanderi* the galley was so narrow I simply bounced back and forth between the stove and sink. My hips were constantly black and blue.

A yacht's stove is usually on gimbals, i.e., suspended so that it can swing. Theoretically, it will remain upright while the boat sails along on its side or bucks and rears. Additionally, most stoves have fiddles—little fences around the edge to keep the pots from sliding off.

But still things can slither and jump and the cook has her hands full just holding the pots in place. Peter solved that problem for us by making adjustable, crescent-shaped stainless steel clamps that kept the pots on the center of the burners. I think they would have worked equally well on a monohull and I don't know why Peter, who was always dreaming of ways to get rich quick, didn't patent that brilliant invention.

PROVISIONING

THE CRUISING LIFE looks carefree, but a yachtie has to think like a quartermaster when planning for a cruise through remote islands or a long passage at sea. The farther he goes from civilization the more self-sufficient he has to be.

The lists! Tools and materials that might be needed for repairing sails, rigging, engine, hull. Medical and first aid supplies. Navigation equipment. Survival equipment. And, of course, food and drink.

Cruising yachts generally carry a lot of non-perishable food. Yachties never know where they'll be shopping next or what might be available or what it will cost, so they try to have enough on board to live for months if necessary. Yachts appear to have little room for storage, but not an inch of space is wasted. Amazing amounts of cans, jars, bottles and boxes come aboard and disappear into lockers all over the boat—under the bunks, settees and floorboards; behind and above seats, toilets, sinks, stoves and iceboxes; onto bunks not needed for sleeping. The icebox itself, rarely used for ice when cruising, is the best storage space for food on most boats—big and conveniently located right in the galley.

Canned foods are the backbone of most yachts' provisions because they're almost indestructible and have an unlimited shelf life. Organized yachties peel off labels, varnish the cans to prevent rust, then label them with a permanent marker. I never took the time to do that and ended up with lots of rusty mystery cans after the labels fell off. Often the dinner menu had to be revised after a can was opened and what I guessed was green beans turned out to be baked beans, three-bean salad or mushroom soup.

I really disliked canned food so we stocked less than most yachties. In the meat department, we liked ham best but considered it too expensive except for special occasions. Spam and corned beef were the only other canned meats we found digestible. In fact they were quite tasty when sliced thin and fried to a crisp.

We also kept a little canned fish on board in case we weren't catching any of the real thing, lots of canned tomatoes and tomato paste because I made a lot of spaghetti sauce and just a few cans of other vegetables and fruit in case we didn't have anything fresh.

I worked hard at always having something fresh to eat, even on long passages. I learned that certain fruits and vegetables kept quite well without refrigeration, even in the tropics. Cabbage, onions, oranges, limes, tropical pumpkin and *chayote* (a prickly, avocado-shaped vegetable called *christophene* in the British islands) lasted for weeks if they had never been refrigerated. And thanks to two sprouters, we had a constant supply of mung beans and alfalfa sprouts. At times we didn't have much variety, but to my mind anything fresh was better than anything preserved.

Dry foods like rice and pasta are wonderful for cruising because they're cheap, filling and don't take up much space. But they don't last long if exposed to moisture and bugs, so airtight containers are a must. We used large plastic coolers with snapping lids for everything we needed to keep dry: spaghetti, macaroni, noodles, rice, instant potatoes, sugar, salt, flour, cereal, beans, crackers, cookies, tea, dried soups and sauces. We did not carry any of those freeze-dried meals packaged for campers and boaters because we found them just about inedible. But we did like instant soups and noodles. They were lifesavers when it was too rough to do anything but boil water.

We stowed a lot of flour because we liked bread. Among the "household" hints we learned along the way: White flour keeps better than dark, and a bay leaf in the flour container keeps the weevils out.

Packaged cereals were prohibitively expensive and bulky, but in New Zealand, the home of do-it-yourself, I learned how to make my own muesli, their favorite breakfast food, by mixing oats, wheat germ, nuts, seeds and dried fruits with oil and honey and "toasting" the mixture in the oven or frying pan for about half an hour, tossing constantly to keep it from sticking to the pan.

We were not milk drinkers, but we kept some aboard for tea, coffee and cereal. We bought powdered milk in tins, the instant variety when available because it mixed so much more easily than the regular. Sterilized milk was also sold in many places where we cruised. It tastes better than powdered but is bulkier, has a shorter shelf life and must be refrigerated after it's opened.

Tinned butter is available in some parts of the world and sounds like a wonderful idea but we found it had often turned rancid before the can was even opened. Margarine kept well, either in cans or plastic tubs, even without refrigeration. It could separate but would return to normal when stirred.

Mayonnaise was not a problem for us because we had a refrigerator. Yachties without fridges were afraid of it spoiling but found it kept perfectly well if untouched by anything but a very clean utensil.

Eggs could be kept for weeks or even months if they had never been refrigerated and if they were coated with something to make them airtight: Vaseline, cooking oil or even varnish.

Frozen foods are rarely a consideration when provisioning a cruising yacht, as most sailors who have freezers find them impractical to use except in port.

What liquid refreshment to keep aboard is a tough decision to make, as none of it is really essential except, of course, for water. Most yachties cannot afford the money or space to stock bottles and cans full of soft drinks, fruit juice, beer and wine. But most of them do find a way when the cargo is liquor. We certainly did.

With the duty-free prices available in some ports, booze is a bargain too good to pass by. When we left the Virgin Islands in 1980, it was possible to buy rum at 99 cents a bottle and vodka at $1.25. *Solanderi* was crammed with food in preparation for the Pacific crossing but, incredibly, we succeeded in stuffing in about a dozen cases of the hard stuff as well.

Peter really preferred beer and when we were in Australia he couldn't resist the opportunity to make his own. The local fad appealed to his pocketbook and his ideal of self-sufficiency.

For an initial outlay of $25 he bought a kit and made 50 bottles of beer. Every month or so he spent another $7 or $8 on the mix and set another batch to brew. The boat smelled like a seedy pub as the stuff bubbled and burped. When it was done, we devoted an entire morning to washing the 50 now empty bottles, rinsing them and sterilizing them, measuring sugar into each of them, filling, capping and restowing them. We always managed to find room for that important cargo.

In the beginning, the beer was so strong Peter would be quite tiddly on two of them, and we had an occasional explosion. We cured both of those problems by cutting down on the sugar.

Some yachties made their own wines but, even though I was a wino, I didn't like the homemade kind. We did make our own coffee liqueur, however, and it was quite palatable, especially if mixed with milk. We had discovered that combination with the store-bought cordial Tia Maria. We called our version Aunt Mary and Milk.

AUNT MARY AND MILK

4 cups water
3 ¾ cups white sugar
2 ozs. instant coffee
26 ozs. cheap brandy or vodka
1 vanilla bean

Boil water. Add white sugar and boil another five minutes. Take off stove, add two ounces of instant coffee slowly, stirring. Bring to a boil again. Remove from stove and let cool five to seven minutes.

Add brandy or vodka. Split vanilla bean lengthwise, put it in a half-gallon jug, and pour the mixture over it. Let it sit at least two weeks. Two months is better. Serve with milk, about half and half.

TO MARKET

DESPITE ALL THE FOOD on board, we were always shopping for more. We ate out of the ship's stores only at sea or when we couldn't find something more interesting ashore.

There's no such thing as one-stop shopping in most cruising ports. Instead we hiked from shop to shop looking for meat at the butcher's, bread at the bakery and fresh food at the market. Rarely did we find everything we wanted but we were easy to please. A pound of stew meat or a head of lettuce was a treat for us.

If we went home empty-handed, we were disappointed but never really surprised. Locally grown food was necessarily limited on small islands and deliveries from elsewhere were unreliable. The supply ships serving the islands were notoriously prone to disasters and almost always late.

The more remote the island, the less there was for sale. In small villages, the "store" was a tiny shack or the front room of someone's home or even the front window of a house. The stock was likely to be a few cans of pork and beans or fish, cigarettes or tobacco, maybe some soap and stale cookies and surprisingly often onions, which don't grow in the tropics. But we always hoped to find them because they made our canned and dry food palatable.

The produce market was the focus of our town shopping because it was fresh food we craved. Some were enormous with heaps of gorgeous fruits and vegetables of all descriptions every day. The prices in these bountiful islands were usually incredibly low—10 or 20 cents for an orange or grapefruit, 50 cents for a few dozen limes. On the lushest islands, fruit was literally given away at the peak of its season. Scroungers like us had free avocados for days in Papua New Guinea because the market vendors didn't bother to carry away the fruit that hadn't been sold at the end of the day.

At the opposite extreme were the very dry islands where there was little to spare. There might have been a weekly market, but the offerings were pathetic and expensive and, too often, sold out within an hour.

We loved the tropical fruits: thin-skinned bananas that are three inches long or two inches around and taste like figs or apples; rich, juicy mangoes, especially the stringless grafted ones, so slurpy we ate them in the sea or over a bucket of water; papayas that were bland until sprinkled with lime juice; pineapples, sweet and sour.

But tropical vegetables are something else. The more primitive societies fill their bellies with an amazing variety of starchy root vegetables—sweet potatoes, yams, taro, cassava. The markets are full of these grotesque tubers—many gnarled and knobby, some hairy, some quite obscene.

We found them all but inedible. Even when we doctored them with margarine, salt and pepper, they remained dry and tasteless. The pretty, round breadfruit which grows on trees was just as hard to make pleasant for us, though we tried every means of preparation we heard about.

We yearned for anything green. In parts of the Pacific, Western-style vegetables were so rare there was only one word for anything green. Now and then we lucked into something from the spinach or lettuce families, but to them it was all "cabbage."

I was shy about bargaining, but in almost every market it seemed we were expected to play the game. The seller set a price well above what the item was worth, we offered half of that and we settled somewhere in between. We often suspected we paid more than the locals did, but cheap as we were we could hardly begrudge the nickels and dimes they charged us.

Thirty dollars was probably the most we spent in a market at any one time. That major outlay was made in the Dominican Republic, a land of plenty, in preparation for a cruise through the Bahamas where fresh food is hard to find. It was a memorable shopping expedition, and even we felt we got our money's worth.

We were shepherded through the vast new market in Puerta Plata by a couple of enterprising street urchins who attached themselves to us and insisted on serving as our guides, translators, bargainers and porters. They led us to an assortment of picturesque market women (a pipe or cigar in each toothless mouth), haggled over prices with them and made sure we got good quality. Our escort increased as our purchases mounted until finally we headed back to the wharf with a procession of six playful brown boys—barefoot, dirty and dressed in rags—marching and yelling through the streets of town with huge loads on their heads and shoulders: Three stalks of bananas in varying degrees of ripeness, 40 pounds of potatoes, 10 pounds of onions, four dozen limes, two dozen oranges, a dozen grapefruit, a couple of pineapples and papayas, lettuce, tomatoes, cucumbers, green beans, cabbage, carrots, radishes and some herbs we couldn't identify, plus coffee, cheese, salami, bread and eggs.

Peter rewarded each boy with a few coins and they, too, were delighted with the deal.

MEETING THE PEOPLE

WE MET THE LOCAL PEOPLE when we traveled on the boat, and I think that is what kept our wanderlust alive. We might have tired of the same old thing—one beautiful island after another—if it hadn't been for the personal encounters. They gave each place some soul, something to remember it by.

For us Raratonga was where we met the princess, a plump, middle-aged woman who rode her motorbike along the waterfront one day and shouted a general invitation to the yachts tied up to the seawall: "Hey, Yank, I'm having a party tonight. Wanna come? I'm the princess. Just ask for the palace."

The princess said she was a descendant of 12 generations of Cook Island kings. Her "palace" was an old, ordinary house with a pretty garden and a pleasant verandah but no kitchen, bathroom or running water. However, she threw great parties.

She loved yachties, especially Yanks, and served a punch called Sailor's Suicide, which was anything anyone wanted to pour into the punch bowl, mixed with fresh orange juice from her orange plantations.

Ofu, a small island in the Vavau group in the Kingdom of Tonga, was memorable for us because that is where we had a very special Sunday dinner with George, the 73-year-old village chief. He cooked for us the traditional way, in an underground oven. The menu was octopus stew, yam and a sweet tapioca dessert, all cooked in coconut milk, all delicious. We sat on the ground outside his hut and spooned the food out of banana leaves but instead of eating native style with our hands, George produced china plates and silverware and there was a flowered tablecloth on the mats. And George, whom we had always before seen toothless, wore a fine set of teeth for the occasion.

I think we were able to make friends with the local people because we fit right in. We bathed in the sea; so did they. We wore T-shirts and flip-flops; so did they. We rowed our dinghy ashore to see them; they paddled their canoes out to see us. They supplied our need for fresh food and water; we gave them store goods in return. We bore little resemblance to ordinary tourists who, with their airplanes, hotels and restaurants, seem to be superimposed on the local scene.

We went to many places where strangers rarely venture. On the more remote islands of the Pacific, the appearance of a yacht in the bay was such an event the entire village turned out to welcome us. Canoes surrounded us and, just like Captain Cook, we were showered with gifts of fruit, but the brown- and black-skinned bodies that swarmed over our sides were more often curious boys than nubile maidens.

The indigenous Polynesians and Melanesians of the South Pacific are renowned for their hospitality and sociability, and we were charmed and delighted by their out-going but gentle style. *But*, the farther west we went the friendlier they became until finally it seemed we had non-stop visitors and no time at all to ourselves.

In Vanuatu and the Solomon Islands, we alternated between enjoying the contact and wanting to be left alone. The people welcomed us without reservation and, apparently assuming that we were as hospitable as they were, they treated our boat as an outpost of their village. Canoes came and went all day, and we often had quite a mob on board. Once I counted 40.

They were polite, well-behaved, and pleased with the sweet candies and powdered fruit juices we offered them but they never wanted to leave, even after we had exhausted all the topics of conversation we could cover with sign language, pidgin and maybe a few words of English.

We discovered that the more primitive people didn't consider conversation a social necessity. They were perfectly happy to sit on our deck for hours just watching us and smiling, giggling or shrieking with laughter at whatever we did. We were the only ones uncomfortable at the lack of verbal communication.

Peter always tried to make the best of any situation and he would spend the long visits learning their language, showing them magazines or letting them watch while he mended a sail or tinkered with a faulty bit of gear.

I was not so adaptable and the literal invasion of privacy made me uptight and cranky. I didn't enjoy preparing a meal in front of an audience, I wouldn't take a bath with people watching and I was damned if I was going to sit on the head while strangers were peeking down the hatch to see what I was up to.

Meals were the biggest problem. The islanders lived a communal life and they prepared a lot of food at one time. Everybody shared and we were always offered something to eat when we went ashore.

But there was no way we could invite our many visitors to join us for a meal and we didn't feel comfortable eating in front of them, so often we starved until nighttime when they finally went home. Then we ate a quick dinner and went to bed, hoping the darkened boat would discourage nocturnal visitors.

We had overdosed on meeting the people. Now all we wanted was to get away from them. We searched the charts for anchorages without villages and were ecstatic if we found an uninhabited island. We couldn't wait to sail to other countries where the natives were less friendly. Of course we missed those lovely people when we were gone, and I wouldn't want to discourage anyone from going there. In retrospect, those stopovers had a quite a lot of charm.

TRADING

TRADING APPEALS TO YACHTIES. They're delighted with an opportunity to hang on to whatever cash they have and pay for things with goods or services instead. We found our best bartering grounds in the outer islands of the Pacific where things haven't changed much since Captain Cook traded trinkets and colorful cloth for fresh fruit.

The people there have little use for money. We met children who had never seen money. On an isolated island in Vanuatu we met a group of young girls who wanted to give us some shells. We had nothing with us to give in return, but Peter found a few coins in his pocket. It was their own currency but they had never seen it before. They were enchanted with the shiny coins but liked the copper pieces (one and two cents) better than the silver (10 and 20).

We traded for fresh fruit, handicrafts and shells. In return we gave canned goods, rice, sugar, tea, tobacco, old clothes, fabric, needles, thread, costume jewelry, magazines, fishing hooks and line, matches, kerosene, soap, flashlight batteries and anything else they needed that we could spare.

Occasionally the trade was for a service. Most islanders have little technical training but are not shy about asking a versatile yachtie to fix things like outboard motors. They're happy to give all the fruit on their trees in return.

Even if Peter couldn't fix whatever was ailing, the people were grateful if he tried. We were invited into a grass hut on a small island in Tonga to look at a "radio no speak." Peter tinkered with it for a while, then had to admit he couldn't fix it. Nevertheless, the grateful family sent us away with our hands full of shells.

Value is in the eye of the beholder, and I often felt we were getting the better end of the bargain. Children brought us armloads of fruit in return for a few cookies or candies. Craftsmen virtually gave away beautiful work if we had something they coveted. In the Solomon Islands we exchanged a pair of old jeans for a pair of wood carvings, and in the Cook Islands we acquired a large, beautifully woven straw mat for a bottle of duty-free scotch, worth about $2.50 at the time.

Many yachties dive for shells and spend endless smelly hours trying to get them clean. We found it much more pleasant to trade for shells that were already cleaned and, since they are as plentiful as coconuts, most islanders put a low value on them. Once we acquired about a dozen magnificent tiger cowries in exchange for an old T-shirt.

Yachties also like to trade with each other. If Peter was repairing a pump, say, and didn't have the right size plastic pipe in his own junk, some other yachtie probably did and Peter was sure to have something the other guy could use in return.

We swapped books and charts with every yachtie we met. It's impossible for a world cruiser to carry all the charts (nautical maps) he might possibly need. Instead he trades along the way, getting rid of the ones he's already used in exchange for the ones he will need next.

Similarly, no yacht can afford the volume or weight of an extensive library. There must be a small, permanent collection of books for navigation purposes, but light reading is normally expendable. Most cruisers carry a limited number of paperbacks and as soon as a book has been read by everyone aboard, it goes into the swap pile. There was very little in the way of great literature acquired in a book exchange but now and then we found a little gem mixed in with the trashy novels and, at least, we always had a new supply of reading material for the next passage.

The cruising fraternity is small enough that we frequently recognized friends' names on flyleaves and now and then had our own recycled books offered back to us, sometimes years later and in a different ocean.

AN ODE TO THE COCONUT

COCONUT PALM TREES are an essential ingredient and the beautiful symbol of tropical islands. It's impossible to imagine the dazzling white beaches and the sparkling turquoise sea without a background of coconut palms and their green, feathery crowns swaying in the balmy breeze.

An ad man's delight. But so much more. Nature outdid herself when she created the coconut palm: It is the ultimate provider.

We always had several coconuts on deck. As the ancient mariners knew, coconuts are the perfect provision: food and drink in one neat, waterproof package that floats and stays fresh for weeks. If necessary, a crew could survive on them alone.

Coconut water, which is the clear liquid inside the shell, is a cool refreshing drink with a slight effervescence to it. It's supposed to be good for the digestive system, and many drinkers swear by it as a hangover cure.

Coconut milk, which is squeezed out of the white flesh of a mature nut, is a marvelous liquid to cook in. In the South Pacific, fish, meat, vegetables and fruit are cooked in coconut milk, or *lolo*, and everything tastes the better for it.

The meat of the coconut can also be eaten as a snack. In younger nuts it is a soft sweet pulp, like jelly. In older nuts it's hard, chewy and rather bland.

My favorite nibbles to serve with drinks are made from the hard meat of the coconut. I called them coco chips and many of *Solanderi's* visitors who thought they didn't like coconut were converted when they sampled these. Here's my simple recipe:

COCO CHIPS

Slice the meat into very thin crescents and let them dry out. Salt the slices and brown them under the broiler or in the oven or frying pan. Eat them right away as they soon turn soggy. Better even than popcorn!

The bad news about coconuts is that it's hard to get at them because the nut is so beautifully protected inside the husk. Peter learned this technique for husking coconuts in the Pacific: Find a stout stick, whittle a sharp point, wedge the other end securely in the ground (or, on a yacht, in a cleat) and plunge the top of the coconut down on the spear in five evenly spaced jabs. Then the husk can be torn off and you're left with a nice brown nut, about five inches long, with three dark spots like the eyes and nose of a small animal.

To get at the water, poke out an eye and pour. To get at the meat, crack the nut open with a rock (or hammer or winch handle). The succulent white meat is firmly attached to the shell, but if you let it dry a while, it will eventually separate enough so that you can scoop it out in reasonably tidy chunks.

To get milk, there's more work to do. I suppose it's possible to grate the pulp in a food processor or blender but the islanders we met did it with a special tool, a piece of furniture in fact, made just for grating coconuts. A rounded piece of metal with serrated edges was attached to a small, squat stool. The cook sat on the stool and rolled half coconuts (still in the shell) over the serrated grater. She caught the gratings in a bowl, added water (the amount varied depending on whether she wanted it thick like cream or watery like milk), then squeezed the mixture through a cheesecloth or handkerchief into another bowl.

We liked cooking with the milk so much Peter made a coconut grater for us, a yachtie version in teak and stainless steel.

The palm trees that supply the coconuts have an impressive list of other uses. A sailor shipwrecked on a tropical island with a few coconut palms could survive quite nicely if he did as the Pacific islanders do. They build huts using the trunks for posts and beams and the woven fronds for roofs and walls, as well as floor mats, hats and baskets. They use the fiber of the husk to make ropes, clothes, brushes and brooms and for starting fires. The shells are used as pots to cook in or bowls to eat and drink from. And there's more: Needles and pins can be made from the tips of the fronds, fishing lures can be fashioned from the tender young shoots, and inside the young trunk is the heart of palm, a salad delicacy.

Finally there's *copra*, the dried meat of the coconut, a cash crop and the only one many Pacific Islanders have. They dry the meat in the sun or over a fire and sell it to traders who sell it to manufacturers of desiccated coconut, cooking oil or soaps and cosmetics.

They also extract some of the oil for their own use as a moisturizer—a strong smelling, glistening veneer for their golden skins.

There's little danger of the islands running out of coconuts. Although the European planters of colonial days abandoned their plantations long ago, the palm trees continue to thrive, producing plenty of coconuts for everyone.

FISHING

OUR FISHING LUCK was spasmodic. We could go a whole passage without a bite or we could catch something every time we threw a line in. Whenever we went to sea we trolled two lines from sunup to sundown, one astern of each hull. We reeled in the lines as soon as it was dark because after that we rarely caught anything but sharks.

Our equipment improved as we went along. Ultimately we were using 200- or 250-pound-test fishing line connected to one of Peter's typically complicated but effective contraptions: an inner tube or a length of surgical rubber as a snubber, a plastic spool as a reel, a bit of wood as a handle for the reel and another stick for the reel to spin on. The stick was attached to a stanchion (a deck post) with hose clamps.

Our lures were whatever the local experts told us "never failed." We tried red feathers in Fiji, silver spoons in the Galapagos, palm fronds in the Carolines and a screwdriver handle in Guam. None of them "never failed."

When we did catch a fish it was all hands on deck to get it aboard. I ran around collecting the necessary gear: a bucket from under the helm seat, the gaff from the tool locker and the big knife from the galley, while Peter hauled the line in hand over hand. Then I helped keep tension on the line by taking up the slack and wrapping it around a winch, cleat or stanchion. When the fish was alongside, Peter gaffed it and wrestled it aboard, then clubbed it with a winch handle or stabbed it with the carving knife.

We caught more tuna than anything and liked it the least. Eventually we learned it was excellent for sashimi (raw, marinated a few minutes in soy sauce or lime juice) and not bad filleted if the dark meat was removed and there was a hollandaise or tarter sauce on the side.

Our favorite fish were wahoo and dolphin—not the porpoise/dolphin but the blunt-headed yellow fish known as *dorado* in Spanish or *mahi-mahi* in Polynesian. In its death throes it is gorgeous, turning iridescent and all colors of the rainbow. Both dolphin and wahoo are light meat, their flavor so delicate I just pan-fried the fillets in a little margarine or oil and served with a squeeze of lime or lemon if I had any.

Most of the fish caught in the middle of the ocean are not designed as dinner for two. They are at least a foot long and weigh at least five pounds. Since we didn't have a freezer, we experimented with other means of preservation, like drying in the sun or pickling in vinegar. Eventually we decided salting was the most palatable method, filling airtight jars with alternate layers of rock salt and thin slices of fish. (If we ran into a bargain on fresh meat we preserved it the same way.) It would keep for months in the brine but required a lot of soaking in fresh water before it was edible again.

We were always wary of fish poisoning and took care to find out which fish were safe in each region. Barracuda carried ciguatera in the Caribbean but were perfectly good to eat in the Pacific, while jacks were poisonous in the Pacific but not the Caribbean. Since the poison is cumulative, we never ate more than three meals in a row from any one fish, just in case.

We always had plenty of other food aboard so that catching a fish was not a matter of life and death for us, but we learned how to fish for survival in the Caroline Islands where they literally live on seafood.

We visited Puluwat and Satawal—renowned as two of the remaining islands in the Pacific where the men still make sailing canoes out of indigenous materials and learn to navigate by the stars, birds and ocean swells.

Tiny specks in the Pacific Ocean, each island is a day's sail from its nearest neighbor and at least 150 miles from a town. Although a supply ship calls more or less monthly with rice and canned goods, the out-islanders, about 600 of them on each island, must be basically self-sufficient.

They grow breadfruit, taro, bananas and, of course, coconuts, and they raise chickens and pigs for special occasions, but their daily diet is based on fish.

Because the waters immediately around the islands were fished out long ago, the fishermen now sail out to sea, to reefs and banks and uninhabited atolls 50, 100 or 150 miles away. Each *proa*—a single hull canoe with one outrigger—is only 25 to 28 feet long but is loaded down with six or eight in crew.

When we sailed in on our relatively huge 45'x20' "double canoe," we were overwhelmed with requests from the locals to take them fishing in our boat. Peter limited the groups to 10 or 12 and our select crews included village chiefs, famous navigators, a Peace Corpsman, a medic and numerous burly fishermen, all clad in brilliantly colored loincloths. I stayed below decks most of the time, because women are considered bad luck on fishing expeditions in the Carolines.

The purpose was to load our decks with as much seafood as we could carry. We sailed 25, 30 and 50 miles to find fishing grounds worth bothering about, then sailed back and forth across teeming banks for hours, trolling at least six lines off the stern, catching an incredible amount of fish, covering the decks with blood and gore.

Our final trip as a fishing boat was a 36-hour marathon from Satawal to West Fayu, an uninhabited atoll abundant with fish, turtles, clams and lobsters.

Our crew for the overnight sail amazed us by arriving drunk. Tuba, a fermented coconut drink, is consumed in vast quantities on Satawal. It was customary, a young man explained to me, to drink enough to forget the problems at home before setting out on a voyage to somewhere else.

While the drunker ones slept sprawled on the decks, the more sober ones took turns at the helm. Much to our disappointment, they stared at the compass all night. We had been looking forward to a demonstration of navigation in the ancient Pacific style.

We arrived at the atoll at dawn and our sobered crew worked steadily until dusk, spear-fishing in the lagoon and diving for clams and lobsters. They filled baskets and baskets full of seafood. Our nets were sagging with it all as we sailed back to Satawal that night, filled with respect for the providers on these isolated islands, thankful that for us a fish was a treat, not a necessity.

NAVIGATION

NAVIGATION TODAY is a breeze if you happen to have electronic help. Just press a button to find out where you are, how far it is to where you want to go, what course to follow to get there and when you can expect to arrive.

Communications satellites have revolutionized cruising for those who can afford hi-tech equipment. First came the satellite navigator (sat nav), now made obsolete by the global positioning system (GPS), an on-board computer that exchanges data with orbiting satellites to pinpoint one's position at any moment anywhere in the world. Designed for ships and aircraft, they have brought yachting out of the 19th century into the space age.

We were in the Pacific when we first heard of sat navs and were amazed at how many yachties were snapping them up. Normally tight-fisted cruisers were laying out a few thousand dollars as if the expensive toy were essential. A small percentage of yachts had radar, which is helpful in coastal navigation, and almost none had loran, which supplies data in the more heavily traveled segments of ocean, but suddenly everyone felt it necessary to have a sat nav.

Peter had neither the money nor the inclination to invest in any of the electronic aids to navigation. Electronics was one field he knew nothing about, and he didn't like having anything he couldn't fix. For that matter he didn't like having anything that might need to be fixed.

The sat navs we knew did need fixing. I assume they improved with time, but in the early '80s they were continually breaking down, and no one could repair them except the manufacturer in London or California. Sat nav owners spent a lot of unwanted time in port waiting for their faulty gadgets to be repaired.

Meanwhile, Peter and I were sailing on the old-fashioned way, relying on the trusty old sextant and the heavenly bodies in the sky to tell us where we were whenever we were out of sight of land. Of course there were times when it was so overcast we couldn't see a heavenly body and would have loved to push a button to find out where we were but, like millions of seafarers before us, we managed to get by.

Celestial navigation takes time and effort but we often wondered what we'd do with the hours at sea if we didn't have navigation to worry about. We already had more time than we wanted to read, sleep, eat and play games.

I dragged my feet about learning celestial navigation. It looked like work to me. But eventually I did it, mainly because I was terrified that Peter might go overboard on one of those long Pacific passages and I would have to sail the boat alone. In fact, it was on the first long Pacific passage that I finally started to learn.

Taking the sights turned out to be harder for me than working out the results. I couldn't wink properly and my hands shook from the weight of the sextant as I tried to capture the sun or a star through the view finder and ever so slowly "bring it down" to rest exactly on the horizon. Accurately recording the split second at which the contact took place was critical for finding our position, but I had trouble even when the sea was flat and the boat steady. When the boat was moving violently and the horizon looked like a mountainous landscape, I could position us right off the chart.

I was better at the paperwork. I had a mental block against understanding the theory of celestial navigation—why the angle of the sun or star at a specific time of day could tell me exactly where I was. I just wanted to know how to find it out. So we concentrated on the procedure—what figures to record, where to find the information I needed in the Nautical Almanac, how to read the tables in "Navigating by the Stars," when to add and when to subtract and, when all the mathematical problems had been worked out, how to transfer the information to the plotting sheet.

I ended up with three typewritten pages of step-by-step instructions for finding our position at sea. I called it "Celestial Navigation for Idiots Like Us." Much to my surprise, I became quite proficient at working out the problems and actually enjoyed the mental exercise with my trusty guide at my side.

The fact that celestial navigation worked, that we always arrived exactly where we wanted to go, remained a marvel and a mystery to me. I shared the wonder of our friend, Don, who re-learned celestial skills on our crossing from Panama to the Marquesas. Every day he shot the sun, worked out our assumed position and X-ed the spot on a chart of the vast Pacific.

We inched along for 35 days without a glimpse of land to verify his findings. When we finally sighted Hiva Oa dead ahead exactly where and when it was supposed to be, he was like a kid, jumping up and down on deck, shouting "It works! It works!"

NAUTICALESE
(AN INFORMAL GLOSSARY)

NOTHING AFLOAT IS CALLED by the same name as it is ashore. From the early days of sailing ships, English-speaking sailors have created a language of their own. I won't attempt to compile a complete dictionary of what I call *Nauticalese*, but here is an informal glossary of the most commonly used nautical terms.

A yacht is full of ropes but not one of them is called a rope. Those used to raise the sails are **halyards**. Those that pull in the sails are **sheets**. The one on the anchor is a **rode**. The one on the **dinghy** or **tender** (the small boat that transports the crew from the yacht to shore) is a **painter**. And all the rest are **lines**—dock lines, furling lines, *etc.*

The front of the boat is the **bow** and the back is the **stern**. To get to the bow you go **forward**, to the stern **aft**. The right side of the boat when looking forward is **starboard**, the left **port**.

The **hull** is the shell of a boat, the structure that floats partially submerged. The part underwater is known simply as the **bottom**, that above the waterline is the **topsides**. (**Topside** is also used as a synonym for **on deck**.)

The **deck** is the horizontal surface on top of the hull. Most yachts have a **foredeck**, **after deck** and two **side decks** straddling the **cabin**, the "house" of the boat. On *Solanderi* we also had a big **centerdeck** between our two hulls.

The tall poles on which the sails are hung are **masts** or **spars**. There are one or two, three or even four masts, depending on the type of boat. The most common are **sloops** and **cutters**, which have one mast, and **ketches** and **yawls**, which have two, the **mainmast** forward and the **mizzenmast** aft. **Schooners** have two or more masts with the mainmast aft.

There is usually another pole, called a **boom**, swinging perpendicular to each mast. A sail is stretched between the mast and boom and is raised, lowered, pulled in and let out by lines led to **winches**, revolving drums that reduce much of the strain. When a line is secured, it is wrapped around a two-pronged **cleat** or snubbed in a **jam cleat**.

Rigging is the overall term for masts, booms and the network of wires that support the masts by connecting them to the hull. Of course they aren't called wires; there are **upper shrouds** from the top of the mast and **lower shrouds** from the **spreaders** (the crossbar about three-quarters of the way up the mast) and there are **forestays** and **backstays**.

I won't go into all the different sails because there are dozens of them. *Solanderi's* "wardrobe" was typical, consisting of a **mainsail**, or **main**, a **mizzen** and the following headsails: **working jib, storm**

jib, **genoa** and **spinnaker**. All of them except the spinnaker were considered essential.

The spinnaker is used only in light airs and when **running**, or sailing **downwind**, *i.e.,* with the wind from behind. The working jib is used when sailing to **windward**, that is, into the direction from which the wind is coming. If the wind is **on the nose**, a sailboat must **tack** back and forth on either side of it, zig-zagging or **beating** its way forward. The genoa is a big jib that can be used when **reaching**, that is, when the wind is on the side, or on the **beam**, or **abeam**. The storm jib replaces all other sails when the weather is so rough that stopping is the best option. The tiny triangle helps keep the boat **hove to**, heading into the wind but going nowhere. (When it's too rough for even a storm jib, the boat has to **lie ahull**, *i.e.,* broadside to the wind.)

The **cockpit** is the sunken sitting area aft of the main cabin where the **helmsman**, or person steering the boat, is stationed at the **helm**, which can be a wheel or **tiller**. A tiller is a long, thin piece of wood which the helmsman pushes in the opposite direction from that in which he wants to go. Both tiller and wheel are connected to the **rudder**, a vertical slab that pivots off the stern and actually turns the boat.

On most modern yachts, the only barrier between the deck and the sea is a thin rail at either end of the boat (the **pulpit** and **stern pulpit**) and **lifelines** (usually plastic-coated wires) along the sides. They are supported at thigh height by **stanchions**, metal rods embedded in the deck. *Solanderi* and most older monohulls also had **bulwarks** or **gunwales**, a foot or more of sides extending up from the deck.

The living accommodations on most yachts are **below decks**, or simply **below**. To get there from the deck you take the stairway or ladder called the **companionway**. The main **cabin** (room) is usually comprised of a **salon** or **saloon** (the sitting and dining area), the **galley** (kitchen), a **head** (both the bathroom and the toilet within) and the **chart table** (a desk where the navigator works). If there are walls separating one area from another they are known as **bulkheads**.

Most yachts are designed with as many **bunks** or **berths** (beds) as can possibly be squeezed in. If there is an aft cabin, it usually houses a master **stateroom** (bedroom) and there is almost always a **V-berth** in the **forecastle** or **fo'c'sle** (bow). There can be upper and lower berths on both sides of the salon and quarter berths tucked under the cockpit.

Hatches are the principal means of ventilation below; an opening in the cabin top is protected by a **hatch cover** which hinges up or slides open to let air in. **Portholes** are small windows in the sides of the hull.

KEEPING WATCH

NON-SAILORS OFTEN ASKED us: "Do you anchor every night?" A naïve question, but what a lovely idea—to stop every evening, go to bed together, and sleep through the night.

Unfortunately, no vessel can carry a long enough anchor chain to reach the bottom of the ocean so when at sea, the boat has to be sailed night and day. Someone has to keep the boat on course, attend to the sails, keep an eye on the weather, look out for ships and, when a landfall is expected, scour the horizon for a dark blob; someone has to be "on watch" each of the 24 hours.

In the old days the watch sat or stood at the helm and actually steered the ship. Now almost every vessel going any distance has some sort of self-steering device. Most cruising yachts have a wind vane attached to the rudder that can be set to keep the boat on course. There are several designs, all costing at least $1,000. Peter made his own, a complicated system of strings and pulleys and cogs and weights and a vane made of two sheets of thin plywood sewn together.

Our vane was christened George. Peter was continually modifying him, and eventually he worked well most of the time. (Interestingly, we met a number of self-steering vanes named George.)

Our George picked up a girlfriend when we were in the South Pacific. Tillie was a different kind of steering aid, an electro-mechanical auto pilot. She was made by a California company, TillerMaster, and Peter went way out character, paying several hundred dollars to buy her new. When the wind was light and/or the boat was under power, George was no help at all but Tillie was marvelous. When the wind was fresh, Tillie was hopeless but George was great. They were a terrific pair.

They relieved us of steering but we still kept a good watch. During the day it was quite informal. If we were both up, we would both have one eye "watching" as we went about our business. But when one of us was napping, the other was in charge.

At night we were more structured. We divided the dark hours into three watches, roughly 9 to 12, midnight to 3 and 3 to 6 a.m. I did the middle shift and Peter took the other two.

I dreaded the night watches; if anything was going to go wrong it was likely to do so at night, when everything was scarier. The wind seemed wilder, the sea rougher, the clouds more menacing than ever during the day. I was nervous and apprehensive charging through the dark, but I had the comfort of knowing Peter was always on call. If there was a squall coming or I thought a passing ship was on a collision course, I woke Peter and he made the decision whether to reduce sail or alter course. I was too insecure to want any responsibility and I was grateful he didn't expect me to take any.

There were nights when he hardly closed his eyes. I worried a lot about his not getting enough sleep, but I didn't hesitate to wake him because no matter how tired he was, he was never grumpy. Peter was a most unusual skipper, asking little from his crew and never reproaching anyone for a mistake. I really appreciated his even temper and his kindness. I would not have lasted a day with many of the captains I knew, who shouted unreasonable orders at their crews and were quick to blame someone else for anything that went wrong.

On uneventful nights when I was relaxed and Peter was able to sleep in peace, my problem was to stay awake and alert during those three long hours.

I was religious about performing my "on watch" duties once every 15 minutes. I checked the compass to make sure we were on course, saw that the sails were drawing properly, checked out the sky for big black clouds that might be squalls coming our way and scanned the horizon for ships' lights.

Then I had to find something else to do. If it was a balmy, clear night I sat on deck, enjoying the moon and stars, listening to Mozart or Neil Diamond on the Walkman. Otherwise, I stayed below where it was warm and cozy.

Solanderi was nicely laid out for long-distance cruising, with all the bunks on the starboard side and the galley and salon on the port side. The crew on watch could have light and sound without disturbing sleepers. I made coffee, worked out the evening star sight and read novels until my eyes rebelled. I also knitted, played solitaire, wrote letters or cooked. Making bread was a good project for a quiet night. I could mix the dough, let it rise, knead it and bake it during my three-hour stint.

When Peter was on watch he made cocoa, worked on navigation problems, read novels and listened to the short wave radio. A true Brit, he loved everything on the BBC, the British Broadcasting Company.

The greatest danger to a yacht at sea is ships. Although sometimes we could go for days, even weeks, without seeing one, we were always alert. The rules of the road state that power gives way to sail, but we were convinced that very few ships kept a lookout and we were doubtful that we would show up on their radar, so Peter's motto was: The big ship has the right of way.

Strangely enough, keeping watch did not carry the same importance on every other yacht. Singlehanders have no choice but to sleep now and then and hope for the best. But, incredibly, we met several couples who told us they both more or less slept through the night. The cruising world is full of hairy stories about yachts colliding with freighters or sailing onto reefs or disappearing without a trace. I find it impossible to understand how a good night's sleep can be considered more important than a lookout that might prevent such a disaster.

CREW

BEFORE MY FIRST long passage I was afraid—of the sea and of how I would handle it. Would I be seasick? Would I get too tired standing watch? Would I be paralyzed with fear if it was rough? I was so afraid of being a washout I thought we should have another crew member aboard. Peter could handle the boat alone, but on a passage he needed someone else to share watches so he could get some sleep.

We were sailing from North Carolina to Tortola, a straight shot, about 1200 miles, maybe two weeks at sea. We took on Bill, a young man who had built a small Wharram cat and sailed it around the coast. He was pleasant and helpful and thrilled at the offer of a free trip to the Virgin Islands. We thought he'd be good crew.

Bill was seasick for three days. I was fine. It was a rough 10-day passage, but I was neither seasick nor exhausted. I was frightened but not petrified with fear. I produced three meals a day, stood my watches, kept a blow-by-blow journal and played nursemaid to Bill.

I was pleased to know that I could handle the responsibilities of crew and I'm sure Peter was, too. From then on, it was almost always just the two of us when we set out to sea.

A yacht owner takes a big chance when he has a stranger aboard. If the crew has ever been involved with drugs, the boat he is traveling on can be suspect. Customs officials can search as thoroughly as they like; they can tear the boat apart if they feel like it. If they should happen to find any drugs on board, the boat can be impounded. No matter how innocent the owner of the yacht, he is the one who loses most. There was no point in our taking any risk. We could sail the boat alone. In fact, we preferred to be alone.

Most couples shared our view, but there were plenty of yachts that did pick up crew, and I'm not talking about the smartly uniformed kind that polish the brass or serve the cocktails on the million-dollar motor boats we called "gin palaces."

Among cruising sailboats, the people who want to crew are usually travelers on a small budget or simply sailors who want to sail. The captains who take them on want extra bodies to share the watches or they need help handling the boat or they hope to make money.

There are probably cases in which the captain pays the crew but in the yachtie world I knew, the exchange went the other way. The crew paid a flat fare or, at least, his share of the expenses.

Whether paying their way or getting a free ride, the crew are generally expected to participate somehow in the ship's routine and most hitchhikers are delighted to do so. Whether peeling potatoes or pulling up anchors, it's all part of the adventure.

The enthusiasm of new crew is good for the old salts who might get jaded otherwise. Our entrance into the Pacific was doubly exciting and meaningful because we had with us our good friend, Don de Socarras, who had dreamed all his life of sailing that first long passage from Panama to the Marquesas. He stayed aboard for the cruise through French Polynesia and he was such perfect crew that after three months together we parted even better friends than when we started.

Unlike most sailors with some experience, Don had the grace to let the captain run the ship. He never suggested that Peter might be wrong, that there might be a better way. He did exactly as he was asked and he was eager to learn whatever Peter could teach him. He was helpful in the galley, too.

When he wasn't being useful or sociable (at meal time and happy hour), he was out of our way, sleeping or reading on his bunk, studying celestial navigation or sitting on the foredeck, gazing into space. On the long pleasant 35-day run from Balboa to Hiva Oa, Don spent hours just looking straight ahead. We never knew if he was thinking deep thoughts or simply "smelling the roses." Whatever it was, we were glad he did it, because soon after he was suffering from throat cancer and three years later he was dead.

THE LONG HAUL
(CROSSING THE PACIFIC)

THE LONG PASSAGE ACROSS the first half of the Pacific, from the Panama Canal to French Polynesia, is many sailors' ultimate dream. Four thousand miles of open ocean, most of it with the tradewinds on the quarter. Weeks out of sight of land. Set twin jibs and never touch them for days. Just glide along, wing and wing, and let the vast, benevolent ocean cleanse your soul.

I'm happy to say that our experience was pretty much as advertised.

We heard of speedy yachts making the crossing in 19 days. And we met a young Frenchman on a 20-foot boat who was out there for

79 days. Our time, 35 days, was about average. (A hundred miles a day is the norm for most yachts on ocean passages.)

We started slowly, hitting the doldrums a few days out of Panama, but there was so much going on around us we were happy to have the time to take it all in.

There were so many porpoises it looked like a convention: tremendous schools of them racing across the ocean as far as we could see and some nights a spectacular show when several of them played around the bows all covered in phosphorescence.

Whales were everywhere—singles, couples and families, swimming, spouting and sounding with a great flourish of flukes, close enough to see well but far enough not to be alarming.

And a seal. Becalmed off the Galapagos Islands, Don made friends with a fat, whiskery seal that played like a porpoise and came within touching distance when Don shone a light on him.

And birds. Dozens of them, circling the boat, playing tag with the sails, or sitting in the water directly in front of us, playing chicken. One cormorant lit on the starboard bow and stayed so long we thought we had a permanent figurehead. Hitchhiking birds are fairly common at sea but, unless they are sick or injured, they are rarely aboard for more than a short rest.

We didn't stop at the Galapagos Islands because yachts were not very welcome at the time (1980) and we didn't want to pay the stiff entry fee or cruise with the required guide on board.

Instead, we crossed the equator, picked up the tradewinds, turned west and sailed straight ahead for the next 3,000 miles.

We quickly settled into a pleasant routine. The boat needed little attention. George (our self-steering device) steered almost all the time. We each stood a three-hour watch at night and spent our days eating, sleeping, reading and navigating.

We were all studying celestial navigation. Peter, who had navigated only by the sun until then and had made do with a hand-me-down aviator's sextant, had a new marine sextant and was learning how to find our position by the stars. Don was re-learning what he had known 25 years earlier as a merchant marine. And I, after seven years of living on the boat, had finally decided it would be a good idea to know how to find out where I was.

Among the three of us, someone was always shooting something—stars at dawn and dusk, the sun morning, noon and afternoon. We found out our position so often it was almost as good as having a computer aboard.

Meals were the high spots of each day. We ate well, with a little fresh food every day, all the way. Not a lot of variety, but luckily we all liked oranges and coleslaw. The weather was so pleasant we almost always ate on deck.

Favorite dinners, all starting from cans or packages, were corned beef hash, chili, spaghetti, fried Spam and mashed potatoes, macaroni and cheese.

Lunch was a *Solanderi* smorgasbord—leftovers and whatever else I felt like putting on the tray. Here is an eclectic luncheon menu I considered worthy of recording in my diary: bread, crackers, caviar, salami, Cheez Whiz, sliced onions, mustard sauce, alfalfa sprouts, cold fried Spam, peanut butter and jelly.

At happy hour we allowed ourselves two drinks apiece and played Scrabble on *Solanderi's* nice stable deck.

Twice we had a little party: a bottle of champagne when we crossed the equator, and wine and South Sea costumes at the halfway mark.

We took bucket baths on deck in the middle of the day when it was warmest. We were all surprisingly modest. Don discreetly went below or looked the other way while Peter and I poured buckets of sea water over each other on the foredeck. We did the same while he had his bath. We each had a final rinse in fresh water, but just a sprinkle. With only 75 gallons aboard for the entire crossing, we counted every drop.

None of us was bored. Only once, early in the passage, when I had read so much my eyes gave out, I noted in my diary that the day seemed to be moving slowly and I wondered what to do with myself next. A week later I complained that I had too much to do: I was exercising every day, making cookies every other day (Don was a cookie monster) and cleaning the boat constantly as mildew settled in. Peter never ran out of odd jobs to do on the boat, and Don was perfectly happy lying in his bunk reading or sleeping or sitting on deck staring into space.

None of us went stir crazy. We didn't get on each other's nerves. We were an unusual trio, all well-suited to the demands of a long sea voyage, each of us enough of a loner to have no problem with the limited company, the lack of outside stimulation or the confined world of the boat.

HEALTH

GOOD HEALTH IS essential in the cruising life. To handle the demands of long-distance sailing and life aboard a small floating home, everyone should at least start out physically fit, mentally alert and emotionally stable. A medical emergency is the scariest of all the hazards to contemplate when setting out to sea and remote corners of the world.

Most cruising yachties are prepared to doctor themselves for routine ailments. They learn first aid and invest in a medical reference book and keep a substantial medicine kit on board with first aid supplies, antibiotics and painkillers, but nothing strong enough to alarm the customs man. A tiny bit of codeine in a cough medicine bottle has been known to cause a lot of trouble.

We all hoped and prayed to avoid an illness or injury we couldn't cure, and that if we had to have one we were in or near a port with decent medical facilities. Hospitals and clinics in the Third World are really basic and they certainly don't practice our Western standards of hygiene. Some of them have dirt floors. Most are thick with flies. There might be chickens running in and out, bloody bandages lying around and no running water.

But we couldn't always avoid them. Like most yachties, Peter and I had a lot of infected cuts, or tropical ulcers. A scrape on coral or rust was likely to develop into a nasty sore requiring treatment with antibiotics. I was also susceptible to ear infections, which also required antibiotics. When our private stash ran out or didn't do the trick, we'd have to get local attention. Depending on the size of the island, the service could be administered by a doctor, a nurse or a medic with about a day's training.

None of them inspired me with a great deal of confidence. I was horrified when a doctor in Vanuatu straightened a paper clip on his desk as a tool for probing in my ear. And I wasn't very happy with the New Guinea doctor who treated a bad sore on my heel, muttering something about gangrene as he whipped out a knife and cut away the rot while Peter held me down.

Dentists weren't any better. In Fiji I chose to live with a toothache rather than be treated in an office strewn with bloody rags. In a capital city in the Caroline Islands I tried again. The dentist there told me how lucky I was that he had any filling material, then proceeded to drill and fill the wrong tooth.

We took every preventive we could get ahold of. In that same town in the Carolines, Peter and I tried to get vaccinated against cholera because there had been an outbreak of the disease in the territory a few months before. But the Public Health Service had only out-of-date vaccine.

Malaria is the big fear in the equatorial Pacific, and we took our anti-malaria pills faithfully every day, starting the prescribed four to six weeks before reaching the infected area and continuing a few weeks after leaving it. But not quite long enough. Peter got impatient with the routine and quit his dosing early. Sure enough, he got malaria.

By then we were in Truk in the Carolines where they didn't have malaria and weren't equipped to diagnose it or to treat it. As self-sufficient yachties, we diagnosed and treated it ourselves with literature and pills we had acquired on the equator, just in case.

I'm no nurse and it was scary for me to have that responsibility, but no way was Peter going into the local hospital. We agreed on that. The treatment he got at home wasn't exactly textbook style, as the nurse spent a lot of time hugging the patient, trying to give him my body warmth during the chills and to draw his heat out during the fevers.

We had the moral support during this ordeal of a young American doctor who made boat calls.

Dick was an ardent windsurfer and every evening after work for the Public Health Service he sailed out to *Solanderi* to check on Peter. As the patient improved, Dick brought his girlfriend, Liz, a Peace Corps nurse, along to visit. They were among the many land-based people we met who dreamed of doing what we were doing.

After their native-style wedding on the idyllic atoll of Puluwat (wearing *lava-lavas* and feasting on roast pig), they went back to the States to make some money so that they could return to the islands in their own boat as mobile, floating medical practitioners.

Dick studied up on malaria when he took on Peter's case, and we were grateful to him for finding out about and dispensing a long-term cure. The medication we had on board zapped the bugs causing the immediate disease. The pills Dick gave us killed the eggs that would have stayed in the liver to cause recurring attacks.

Who knows what would have happened if Peter had been taken ill in the middle of the ocean? I never wanted to even think about an evacuation at sea, but when there is a serious illness or injury on board and medical attention is required but is days away in terms of sailing time, the patient should be moved to speedier transportation. But it's not that easy. *If* the yacht is able to make radio contact with a rescuer, and *if* a ship or helicopter is able to find the yacht, then a genius is required to engineer the transfer.

The problem is the mast or, even worse, masts plural. A sailboat has at least one constantly swaying, 30- or 40- or 50-foot long stick in the middle of the boat, with wires radiating from the top of it like a maypole. To pluck a disabled person from the sailboat's rolling deck to a helicopter hovering overhead or a ship looming alongside, without getting entangled in the rigging, is an extremely difficult operation.

Most yachties wouldn't risk damaging their boats except for a matter of life or death, so most of the rare evacuations we heard about were for heart attacks or broken necks.

SEASICKNESS

MANY YACHTIES SUFFER from seasickness. It isn't necessarily something that goes away with time. A surprising number of people who have been cruising for years get sick every time they go to sea, not just once but continuously, for days. Why they keep going is beyond me. My sailing career would have ended abruptly after the first barf.

There are chronic cases who turn green just looking at a boat, any boat. Others are more selective. Some can handle sailboats but not motorboats, and vice versa. Some can sail on multihulls but not monohulls, and vice versa. Some are better on big boats, others on small. Every vessel has a different motion.

Obviously, the afflicted ones cannot sail alone. They must have kind-hearted crew willing and able to take over their duties when they're doubled up over the rail.

Fortunately, medical researchers are working hard on cures for motion sickness, and I'd certainly recommend that a "poor sailor" keep trying whatever's available in hopes of finding something that works for him. Nothing is worse to me than being seasick.

There are many brands of motion sickness pills, and some of them have followers who won't set sail without them. But pills often have the side effect of drowsiness, which makes them impractical for many sailors.

Ear patches seem to do away with that problem but can cause another. Small patches that are stuck behind the ears and are replaced every few days let medication be absorbed slowly through the skin. Many patch users are thrilled to feel no nausea or drowsiness, but some complain that their eyesight is affected, that they have trouble focusing—again, an unacceptable side effect for a yachtie who must be able to read charts and navigation tables or who wants to while away the hours with a good book.

The latest discovery to be hailed with enthusiasm by seasickness sufferers is a pair of bracelets called Sea Bands, which apply pressure to the wrists' pulse points and somehow, miraculously, make the nausea go away. So far I haven't heard of any adverse reactions to this form of acupressure, and of course I don't know if it works for everyone, but maybe, hopefully, at last, seasickness can really be cured.

Many sailors who don't actually get sick do feel queasy until their bodies adjust to the motion of the boat. Their temporary condition doesn't often require doctoring, just time and common sense, avoiding anything that makes the nausea worse.

I was lucky. I never threw up. I could get queasy and not be interested in food, but if I could lie down for an hour or more I'd usually feel okay. Often a few soda crackers settled my stomach and sometimes a snort of medicinal whiskey helped, both taken while horizontal. I could even read. If I slept a little that was good. Soon I'd be up and feeling fine again.

In the beginning of my cruising career, when I was afraid of being sick, I tried pills for motion sickness. One pill would knock me out and I couldn't shake off sleepiness entirely for about 24 hours, an impossible situation when you have to be on watch half of the time. I preferred to do without, and luckily I found I didn't really need them.

Although Peter considered himself immune to *mal de mer*, there were times when even he came running up on deck for air. What got to him was trying to read fine print like that in the navigation tables when the weather was rough and the boat was in constant motion.

Our first-hand experience with seasickness was thankfully limited, but nevertheless we learned what to do, just in case.

Stay in the fresh air. It that doesn't help or if it's too cold or wet on deck, go below and immediately lie down. The lack of fresh air below decks can make you feel sicker, but there's something about being horizontal that relieves the nausea.

Try to avoid galley smells and engine smells. Keep warm. Try to relax. Try to sleep.

If you're hungry or feel you should try to eat, nibble a soda cracker or piece of bread while still horizontal. Sometimes hunger and seasickness create similar sensations in the stomach and a bite to eat is all that's needed to cure you.

Drink a minimum of liquids. They slosh around in your stomach as the boat plays rock and roll. Coffee and tea, the sailor's constant companions, are especially hard on a delicate gut.

If passive resistance doesn't work, try pills or patches or wrist bands.

If you still succumb, please remember a most important point of yachting etiquette: *Don't throw up to windward.*

FORMALITIES

CRUISERS SPEND a lot of time doing "the formalities," officially entering and clearing port. Procedures vary from country to country, and we never knew what to expect next.

At one extreme was a Banana Republic scenario in the Caribbean, where we were boarded by eight gun-toting toughs in khaki. At the other extreme was a tropical paradise scenario in French Polynesia, where we dealt with a laid-back official whose "uniform" was running shorts and a T-shirt imprinted GENDARME. In between, we met a lot of routine government employees who simply shuffled and stamped a lot of papers.

Paperwork for a yacht is, alas, the same as for a freighter or ocean liner. Almost everywhere we went Peter had to fill our reams of forms full of irrelevant and often obsolete questions such as how many tons in ballast and how much coal we carried! There were always forms for customs and immigration officials, and there were sometimes additional papers for a health official, an agricultural inspector, a port captain, a policeman and/or a soldier.

Traditionally, a vessel is quarantined on arrival in a port; no one can go ashore until all the authorities have stamped and signed all the pertinent documents and the customs man, if he wants to, has searched the boat for contraband. We must have looked harmless because only once did we have more than a superficial inspection. Less lucky yachts have been torn apart when there was a suspicion of drugs aboard.

Once the authorities have given permission to go ashore, sailors can take down the yellow quarantine flag that has been flying from the spreaders (a cross beam on the mast) since they arrived in port. Proper etiquette is to replace it with a courtesy flag, a small copy of the flag of the country being visited.

It's possible to buy courtesy flags from yachting suppliers, but that was not Peter's style. Instead, he assumed that I was perfectly capable of making reasonable facsimiles from whatever rags and scraps of material we had aboard. I begrudged the hours of effort required to sew tiny white stars, say, onto a red square, and to make it look the same on both sides. When I became smart enough to substitute ink and glue for some of the sewing, both my disposition and my flags improved.

In many of the countries we visited, formalities were so casual we could have come and gone unnoticed. But since we needed to clear one country in order to enter the next, Peter had to flush out the officials if they didn't come to us. They were usually spread all over the island. The port captain might be near the port but the customs official was probably at the airport and the immigration man at an office in town. Sometimes it took all day to enter.

When we had guns on board, our paperwork—and our footwork—was endless. Peter started his yachting career with a rifle and a shotgun, expecting to do a lot of hunting, which he never did. But he dutifully declared the guns in every port. It was too risky not to; if the boat was searched and firearms were found, the penalty could have been a very unsavory jail stay.

The guns always required extra forms to fill out and sometimes two visits to the police station, one to turn them in and one to get them out. In Jamaica we went through this rigmarole in every port, and we were moving every few days. It didn't leave us much time to enjoy the island. After that Peter gave the guns away.

They would not have helped us as weapons of self-defense. To keep them from falling into hostile hands, we kept them so well hidden it was quite a production to get our own hands on them. Instead we relied on our flare guns in case we ever needed to defend ourselves. They were not considered firearms so did not have to be declared and, because we thought the average burglar wouldn't recognize their potential as weapons, we felt safe enough keeping them readily accessible.

A small percentage of the countries we visited required visas, rather difficult to acquire when we were cruising in remote areas, but we became quite good at planning our routes to include towns with embassies and consulates. The fees were generally quite reasonable, $15 or so.

If visas weren't required, we rarely paid anything to enter a country. A notable exception was French Polynesia, which required a bond worth the price of airfare back to our countries of origin. They must have had a lot of undesirable yachties going native to have come up with such a stiff assessment; in 1980 it was $850 for me to the U.S., $1,600 for Peter to the U.K.

The only other money I can remember paying an official was in a Central American port where each of six men in the boarding party went away with $5. We never knew whether the government received the money or the officials pocketed it. Either way it's quite remarkable that it happened only once.

HURRICANE SEASON

IN THE TROPICS, six months out of every year, hurricane season interrupts cruising—from June through November in the northern hemisphere, from December to May in the southern hemisphere. Yachties who stay in a hurricane belt either hole up for the season or cruise close to shore, with an ear tuned to the weather forecasts and an eye on the charts, always looking for the nearest safe harbor in case they have to duck in. Long passages are out of the question; they don't want to be caught at sea with nowhere to go.

Except for its name, a hurricane in the Atlantic or Caribbean is the same thing as a typhoon in the North Pacific, Indian Ocean or South China Sea. It's also the same as a cyclone in the southern hemisphere, except that there the winds swirl in the opposite direction.

Whatever it's called, a cyclonic storm is a terrible threat to a yacht. When winds of more than 75 miles an hour, rough seas and unusually high tides combine forces, boats can be sunk, smashed against rocks, reefs or other vessels, or left high and dry many feet inland.

Few cruising yachts are insured, as the cost is prohibitively expensive to anyone without a steady and sizable income.

To avoid the possibility of losing their homes, many yachties leave the tropics, at least for the season, heading for the equator or the higher latitudes where hurricanes aren't supposed to happen.

We tried all the options. In the South Pacific we spent two seasons out of the path of cyclones, one cruising near the equator in the Solomon Islands and Papua New Guinea, where it was too hot, and another in New Zealand, on the other side of the storm belt, where it was too cold.

We loved the tropical climate and, despite the constant vigilance required for half the year, we preferred to stay in our chosen latitudes, between 15 and 20 degrees. Sometimes we cruised but generally we stayed more or less put for the season. Peter found a job, we worked on the boat, we flew to the States and England to see our families and sometimes we traveled ashore.

I liked hurricane season; I was relieved to know I wouldn't have to go to sea for a while. I enjoyed being in one place long enough to get to know my way around town, to join the library, to take an art class, to feel a part of a community.

Hurricane holes aren't pleasant anchorages. The very qualities that make them safe harbors in storms also make them hot, airless, buggy and muddy. So we generally anchored where there was a breeze and clear water, but with a refuge nearby. As soon as we heard of a storm heading our way, it was out of the open bay and into the hurricane hole: a river, creek, lagoon or well-protected bay, anywhere not likely to be affected by a fetch, or build-up of the seas.

Some seasons we never had to run for shelter, others we did it half a dozen times. Only twice did we actually get hit. In 1985 Typhoon Bill passed close enough to Guam to give us 80-knot gusts, but we were at the tail end of a winding creek, securely tied to pine trees all around. We felt no seas at all and hardly any wind.

We had learned our lesson 10 years earlier in St. Maarten, in the West Indies, where we negligently got taken by surprise and had to ride out Hurricane Eloise on one anchor, in between two reefs. It was pure luck that our anchor held. We could easily have ended up on coral or the beach, where two other yachts came to a splintery end.

Multihulls have a big advantage over monohulls when securing for a storm and, after our one lapse, we were careful to make the best of it. With *Solanderi's* shallow (three-foot) draft, we could hide from the elements in swampy little corners, put out a cat's cradle of lines to the mangroves or trees ashore and not have to depend on anchors or moorings at all.

If we wanted to go away during the hurricane season, we felt safe leaving the boat in such a spot.

During our "vacations" (when your life is a vacation, what do you call time off?) we continued to live like vagabonds. We simply switched from the boat to a car as our means of travel.

We never invested in real camping gear. We simply bought or rented a vehicle we could sleep in, moved our sleeping bags and cooking things from the boat to the car and hit the road.

I longed for a touch of luxury now and then, but Peter in a hotel or fancy restaurant was a duck out of water. Not that he didn't know how to behave, but he felt so uncomfortable with servants hovering about him and he was so unhappy parting with all that money, we were better off camping out.

STORMY WEATHER

BY PETER'S DEFINITION, I was never in a storm at sea. When the frothing waves looked storm-size to me, Peter shrugged them off as maybe 10 or 12 feet. When the wind shrieking through the rigging sounded like a hurricane to me, Peter would guess 35, maybe 40 knots. We had no way to measure either phenomenon accurately and Peter made conservative "guesstimates." He was a rare captain who liked to minimize the drama.

Most sailors tend to exaggerate. They routinely talk and write about gale-force winds and 20-foot swells. If they're long-distance cruisers they're likely to have at least one good storm story to tell: they've broached, been pooped, knocked down or dismasted or at the very least limped into port with broken rigging.

111

We managed to sail around intact for 13 years, but we had our share of rough weather and I lived in fear of a disaster.

When it was rough, *Solanderi* had an unsettling repertoire of violent motions: shaking, jerking, pitching and lurching. We would be flung around the cabins or bounced off the bunks every time a big wave slammed against the side, and the pounding and banging of the seas against our plywood hulls was deafening. There were times when it felt and sounded as if we had just smashed into a concrete wall. I wondered if the boat could take all that punishment. I worried that a side would come crashing in. I worried that the boat would break up.

I also worried about me. My heart lurched when the boat lurched and continued to race as I waited to see if we were still in one piece. My stomach was a nervous knot when I watched Peter on deck doing what had to be done: reducing sail, adjusting the steering vane, lashing down the dinghies and other loose objects. He didn't wear a safety harness and I was terrified he would be swept overboard. If I had to do something, like steer, I shook so hard I could hardly move.

Every time we went through stormy weather I vowed never again. I swore it was my last passage—but only to myself. I was insecure enough to worry that if I said it out loud, Peter might jump at the opportunity to get rid of me. And once the danger was past, once we were safely in port, I knew I would rather live with fear than live without Peter.

Cruisers have an adage about long-distance sailing, that it's "hours of sheer boredom punctuated by moments of sheer terror." I could certainly relate to that, but not Peter. He was easily bored ashore but never on his boat, and he was too much of a survivor to have time for fear. His response to an emergency was action, or reaction. He seemed to know instinctively what to do, how to cope, how to remedy the problem, and he never stopped working until the danger was past.

Peter was one of those sailors who loves to be at sea no matter what. Even when wet, cold and tired, he remained cheerful. Even when all hell broke loose, he remained cool. His boat was an extension of himself and his life was a series of successfully met challenges to his seamanship and his yacht's seaworthiness.

Peter's image of the perfect mate was, naturally, a woman who shared his love of the sea. Once, early in my life aboard, I candidly admitted to some friends that I didn't like sailing when it was rough. Peter looked so surprised, disappointed and embarrassed by my revelation I tried never to mention my weakness again. Although he knew I didn't live up to his image, I think he tried to deny it, even to himself, certainly to other people. And I went along with the lie.

SURVIVAL

MULTIHULLS ARE NOT SUPPOSED to sink, and I put a lot of faith in *Solanderi's* buoyant construction and watertight bulkheads. I cherished the belief that she would float even if she turned turtle or had a gaping hole in the side. I envisioned us surviving indefinitely on our "raft." Whether the boat was wallowing or was upside down, we could dive into the galley for food and water while waiting for rescue.

A comforting scenario, but still there was the possibility the boat could break up if the damage was extensive enough. It we had to abandon ship, we needed a life raft.

Our life raft (a gift from my mother) was a round rubber double tube that lived in a nylon "valise" on deck. If we ever had to launch it, we were to pull a string which would release a canister of compressed air and the raft would break out of the box fully inflated. It had a high-visibility canopy colored international orange to attract the attention of passing planes or ships and to protect us from the elements. A small survival kit that came with the raft included about six cans of water, a few flares, a small metal mirror for signaling to would-be rescuers and a small box of first aid supplies.

After reading a couple of fabulous survival stories—thirty-some days in a life raft, a *hundred*-some days in a life raft—we put together our own greatly expanded survival kit, a five-gallon airtight, waterproof plastic container stuffed with fishing hooks and line, more medical supplies, concentrated high protein food bars, malt tablets and whatever else occurred to us over the years. Some yachties included passports and travelers' checks in their grab bags.

If we ever had to abandon ship our plan was to load the life raft with the survival kit, as many plastic water jugs as we could handle (we always left an inch or so of air space at the top so that they would float) and the EPIRB. The Emergency Positioning Indicator Radio Beacon (another gift from my mother) is a gadget the size of a fire extinguisher that transmits a distress signal to ships and planes up to 150 miles away. I counted on it a lot, but in the middle of the vast Pacific I couldn't help but wonder if anyone would be close enough to hear our call.

Many yachties are very radio-oriented and consider their two-way radios—VHFs, single-side bands and ham sets—as emergency equipment. If disaster strikes, they reach for their radios and call for help. Peter considered this a waste of precious time; he would be too busy trying to save the boat to issue a "May Day," the call that says "I'm sinking. Please come rescue me." Eventually he did invest in a ham radio, mainly to keep on top of the weather and other conditions affecting cruising. Although he never admitted that he might depend on it to save his life, I was certainly relieved to know we had another chance of making contact in an emergency.

Next to the boat's sinking, the worst calamity that can happen at sea is for someone to go over the side.

The man-overboard drill is part of every sailor's basic training. The assumption is that if anyone does go over, there are others on deck to toss him a life ring, release the man-overboard pole (a long stick with a flag and strobe light on top to mark the spot), turn the boat around, sail back alongside the one in the water and help him get back aboard.

It's a difficult maneuver, even in classroom conditions. In the open sea, the chances of a successful rescue are slim. *If* someone is on deck to see the man go overboard, *if* he reacts immediately and does everything perfectly, he still might not find the victim. Even the longest man-overboard pole is quickly lost to view in moderate to large swells.

So most sailors don't put a lot of faith in man-overboard drills. They concentrate on prevention instead. Some skippers have strict rules about everyone on deck wearing a safety harness at all times, plus a life jacket when it's rough. Others use the harness only when it's rough, or at night, or when they have to go forward.

The harness wraps around the upper torso and is attached to a line with a clip on the end. As the sailor moves around the boat he clips himself to the lifeline, the mast or boom or whatever's handy to his work. On monohulls especially, when the boat is heeled over at a 45-degree angle, or when a sail change has to be made on the pitching bow, the crew must have a reliable harness to keep him on the boat.

Peter wore his only if he had to climb the mast. Because *Solanderi* didn't heel and because she was 20 feet wide, he felt safe enough without one.

I worried constantly about his going overboard because, to adjust the self-steering, which he did often, he had to lean out over the stern while fending off a wildly swinging tiller. I was out of my bunk often, especially on rough nights, checking to see if he was still around.

If Peter had gone over, I didn't expect to be brave. Although I had learned celestial navigation just in case, I really didn't see myself trying to sail the boat alone for any length of time.

I would have been too busy trying to operate the radios, calling for help.

KEEPING IN TOUCH

KEEPING IN TOUCH with the folks back home and with other cruising friends brought us into frustrating contact with the real world. Mail moved slowly in and out of remote ports, and we couldn't just pick up a phone and dial.

Our cruising years pre-dated fax machines and e-mail. How I envy the yachties today. Our communications choices were limited to the post and phone.

Our correspondence was a stamp collector's dream but often caused us nightmares. We'd leave one place before our mail got there and arrive at another after it had left. Letters could follow us around for months, and God knows how many were lost—forwarded to somewhere we didn't get to or carried to a rendezvous that never happened. One Christmas we enjoyed a big bundle of cards that had been written to us the previous season. They had been chasing us around the Pacific for a year.

Yachties depended on each other for personal delivery of mail. Postmasters, even when given more than adequate money for postage, never forwarded our mail from one country to the next. Instead they stamped it unclaimed and returned it to the sender. By slow, slow boat. My mother had letters returned six months to two years later.

Probably the most efficient way to handle incoming mail is to have it all sent to a reliable friend or relative back home who collects it and bundles it and waits for the yachties to send a safe address. Even that doesn't always solve the problem because one of the givens of cruising is that all plans are subject to change—due to the weather, a problem with the boat or the whim of the sailors.

The telephone was a much more satisfactory means of communicating long distance but it wasn't always easy to find one. I know, because I tried to call my mother on a regular basis.

My mother was a worrier and my going to sea in a small sailboat was torture for her. She needed to hear my voice frequently to be sure that I was still alive. I could empathize, and I tried to call her every two weeks. The search for a telephone sometimes put quite a strain on our carefree lifestyle, as not every atoll has one, and when I couldn't find one I worried about my mother's worrying about me. Peter was remarkably tolerant when I got uptight about calling her and always did his best to get me to a phone when the time came.

In a couple of remote outposts, my attempt to telephone the U.S. was the local event of the year. In a small town in the Dominican Republic the event took place in a tin shack that housed all the government offices and several beds. The "Communications Department" was one antiquated telephone in a back room with the receiver hooked up to an amplifier in the vain hope that something would be heard.

In the Solomon Islands, after looking for a phone for a month, we finally sailed into a government station that had a radio-telephone for emergency purposes. I was desperate enough to try anything, and the radio man was kind enough to help me out. The call had to be relayed through Honiara, the capital. Amazingly, Mum and I were connected, we could hear each other and the operator obligingly switched us on and off, even when we forgot to say "Over."

It was easier, but not much, when we got to civilization. Most towns had a telephone office with an operator and one or two international lines. Some were fairly sophisticated, with private booths, waiting rooms and speedy connections. But more often there was a long wait without a place to sit, no privacy and such poor connections it was difficult to transmit much information. However, as long as we could assure each other that everything was fine, we were happy.

Some offices would take only cash. Others would place only collect calls. Rarely did I find an operator who would use my calling card, or even know what it was.

The offices were open only during business hours, which meant that with my calling from as much as 12 time zones away, my mother heard my cheery hello at some very ungodly hours.

Telegrams were mysteriously disappointing. On a few occasions when I tried to substitute a cable for a call and was assured the message would be delivered in a matter of hours, or certainly days, I later found out the wire took as long as a letter. Incoming telegrams were no better; they also disappeared into the void, arriving two weeks after they were sent.

Some yachties avoid the hassle of public communication by using amateur radios. They have a ham set on board and the parents or children have one at home and they make an agreement to talk to each other at a certain time every week or month. For some families, this works fine.

Not for mine. Even if I and my 80-year-old mother had been capable of mastering radio transmission, there was the possibility that I might not "come up" at the appointed hour. The radio could break down, I could forget, we could be lost ashore or in the middle of a crisis at sea. But whatever the reason, my worrying mother would have jumped to her own conclusion. For her it could only have meant that *Solanderi* had sunk.

WATER

WATER, WATER EVERYWHERE—but it's all salty.

Fresh water is a constant cause of concern on a boat. The supply is limited but must be made to last until replenishment can be found, and no one ever knows for sure when that might be. Catastrophe is to run out of fresh water at sea.

Despite the importance of the precious commodity, most cruising yachts carry little of it for the usual reasons of weight and space. A hundred gallons is probably about average. Many households go through that much water in a day quite casually. It's amazing how long it can be made to last when necessary, and when there's an endless source of salt water within arm's reach that can be used for most jobs—washing the decks, the dishes and the people, and flushing the toilets, or heads.

Solanderi carried only 75 gallons of fresh water, but even on long passages and even when there were three of us aboard, the minimal supply was adequate. Of course we didn't waste a drop.

Here's how we bathed when we were anchored in clean water: We jumped over the side to get wet, came back on deck for a sprinkle of fresh water to soap up in (we used shampoo on our bodies as well as our hair because it sudsed better than soap), jumped back in to rinse off the suds, then climbed aboard again for a final fresh water rinse. A two-liter jug of fresh water was plenty for both of us.

If there were people nearby, we had our baths modestly, wearing bikinis. We entertained a lot of spectators with our curious ablutions.

If the water was too dirty, or the air was too cold, we made do with sponge baths below in the starboard cabin where we had a small basin in our "dressing room."

Many yachts have built-in showers, but homemade *Solanderi* did not. Eventually Peter did create a typically makeshift system by which we could have a shower if we felt it was worth the trouble to assemble the parts: a shower curtain to encircle the bather and keep the cabin dry, a plastic tub to stand in, a recirculating pump attached to a length of plastic hose and a shower head clipped to an overhead beam. If we wanted to really live it up and have a hot shower, we heated the kettle on the stove in the port cabin, carried it up one ladder, across the deck and down another ladder to the starboard side. I don't think it ever occurred to me to question why we didn't rig the shower on the side with the stove!

When we were at sea we usually had bucket baths on the foredeck. Boat people attach five or six feet of rope to all their buckets so that they can haul salt water from the sea to the deck. There's a knack to filling a bucket this way: While hanging on to a loop in the end of the line, you toss the bucket down with a bit of a flick so that it lands in the water upside down. Then you pull on the rope until the bucket is upright and full of water, and you haul it up to the deck without tilting it so that all the water stays in. It's quite a trick, even in a calm anchorage. When the boat is moving, the hauler also has to contend with the force of the ocean's resistance as the bucket is dragged through the sea. It was stronger than I was and after losing a few buckets I gave up. Peter had to be my waterboy at sea.

We squandered quantities of seawater for washing dishes as well as for baths.

At anchor, I usually did the dishes on deck, surrounded by buckets full of salt water. Last night's dinner dishes had been soaking in a bucket overnight, as I hate to end a lovely evening by washing dishes. But it was a morning ritual I enjoyed, taking it slowly, gazing around at the view. By the time I emptied the dirty water over the side the tradewinds had blown everything dry.

We lost only a few utensils that way, but we almost lost everything when a guest volunteered to help. Our friends, Queenie and Don, were visiting us in the Bay Islands of Honduras when Queenie, a helpful guest, one morning after doing the dishes poured all our knives and forks over the side. Luckily, we were anchored in only 15 feet of clear water and Peter and Don were able to retrieve everything in a few dives. It was a scene from the twilight zone as they surfaced with hands full of stainless steel cutlery, shiny bounty of the deep.

I allowed a tiny bit of fresh water for a final rinse. Without it, the dishes retained a damp, salty film.

Joy, by the way, was the only detergent we found that really sudsed well in salt water.

Our galley (or kitchen) sink had both fresh and salt water. The fresh water was pumped from our only water "tank," actually a modified 12-gallon plastic jug. The salt water was pumped directly from the sea.

Some yachts are equipped with household faucets, but most cruisers prefer either hand pumps or foot pumps because there are fewer things to go wrong and there is less chance of wasting the liquid gold.

If the seawater was clean, we used it even for cooking. Most cruising cookbooks say you can cook in half and half, salt and fresh; we found that much too salty a solution. One-fourth salt water was more to our taste, but even that small saving of fresh water was considered important.

On the rare occasions when we were anchored in a harbor of dirty water and I had to use fresh water for washing the dishes, I invented a new procedure. I simply rubbed the dirty things with a wet soapy sponge and rinsed them in a big salad bowl with just a couple of inches of water in the bottom.

Most yachts have built-in tanks for both fresh water and fuel. As usual, *Solanderi* had a simpler and cheaper way. We stored all our liquids in plastic jugs. Our 75 gallons of fresh water were distributed among a few five-gallon jerry jugs, the 12-gallon "tank" and numerous two-liter wine jugs that had come with the boat.

I spent a great deal of time juggling the jugs, siphoning from large to small, from portable to stationary. We usually collected water on deck in the five-gallon jugs, then transferred it. The small containers were a handy size to pour from and we kept them lined up under the sinks.

Replenishing the water supply is a continuous chore. At anchor, the self-sufficient yachtie catches rain water on his boat, from cabin tops, decks and awnings.

Peter's catchment system was the most efficient I ever encountered: a large awning with sewn-in funnels that plugged into plastic tubes that ran into jerry jugs on deck. The briefest of showers could net us a few gallons of water and we could be miles away at the time.

If it didn't rain we had to get water ashore. Boats with big tanks will fill up at a dock, if there is one. For our small supply it wasn't worth the trouble of going alongside. Instead we piled our jerry jugs into the dinghy and filled them wherever we could. If we were anchored off a town or yacht club there was usually a tap not too far from where we went ashore. But on small islands the source of water might be a well or a stream, and it might be a considerable distance from the beach. Our five-gallon jugs weighed 40 pounds when filled with water. I couldn't carry them more than a few feet but there were often local boys around who were happy to struggle with a jug in return for some small present or a visit to the boat. Peter was happy to let them help but he had a problem accepting women as workhorses, which was the cultural attitude in many Pacific countries.

On one small island in the Solomons, where we arrived ashore with four five-gallon containers, four women accompanied us to a well in the center of the island where they slowly filled the jugs, using a tea kettle and a coconut shell as dippers. That was fine, but when they hoisted the filled containers onto their heads for the half-mile walk back to the dinghy, Peter protested. His objections were ignored by everyone—by the women who walked along at a steady pace, apparently comfortable enough, and by the men and boys who strolled by their sides, empty-handed.

GARBAGE AND SEWAGE

SAILORS HAVE A UNIQUE DILEMMA when disposing of waste, both garbage and sewage.

There may be laws dictating proper disposal procedures in a few civilized ports but, generally speaking, yachties are on their own and they follow two sets of unwritten rules—one for anchorages and another for the open sea.

In the middle of the ocean, all sewage and most garbage go directly into the sea. Environmentally caring yachties save their plastic bags and other never-biodegradable rubbish for eventual disposal ashore, but few of them have the space or inclination to store used cans and bottles until they find a proper dump. We were careful to insure that nothing we tossed over the side would float for very long—uncapping bottles and jars, puncturing cans, *etc.,* so that everything would go directly to the ocean floor.

I was horrified at the idea of littering the ocean when I started cruising, but I soon discovered that our method of waste disposal was more ecologically responsible than that of many island governments.

On my first cruise, after saving all our garbage for days, at my insistence, we finally hauled bags full of rubbish to a trash barrel on the dock in the French island of St. Bart's (St. Barthelemy). As we left the island, rounding a cliff on the lee side we saw an avalanche of garbage spilling from the point into the sea. We had discovered the island dump. A garbage truck was parked on top of the cliff and a couple of men were tossing the day's trash, probably including ours, directly into the sea, plastic bags and all.

We sailed slowly westward with a vast train of garbage bags bobbing gently in our wake. Many fish, birds and turtles probably dined on St. Bart's refuse that day (and every day). The quantity of plastic served them was enough to cause numerous stomach aches and probably a few deaths.

When we were anchored, we naturally took almost all our rubbish ashore. Most yachties don't litter their own backyards. But readily bio-degradable garbage like leftover food almost always went over the side after dark. The fish dined well, and the anchorage was spotless for those who wanted to swim or bathe or admire the crystal clear water the following day.

Floating rice and beans may be an aesthetic turn-off, but it's nothing compared to an encounter with human turds during one's morning swim.

In most cruising harbors, the sewage generated by the boats at anchor goes directly into the water. Marine toilets (heads) are flushed with seawater pumped from under the boat into the bowl and back out again. In idyllic harbors pollution is not a problem; the tides provide a natural flushing action, leaving the water clean enough for swimming, bathing and washing dishes. But in crowded anchorages or bays where the water does not circulate well, boats rock gently in cesspools of their own creation. It's a problem—medically, environmentally and aesthetically.

The United States has addressed the problem by requiring holding tanks installed in every vessel, similar to those in camping vehicles. Theoretically, all the contents of all the heads are treated chemically and stored in tanks; when full, the tanks are pumped out at pumping stations ashore or miles out at sea. Hopefully the system works for new American yachts cruising in American waters.

But that law doesn't affect most cruisers. Yachts built in other countries or American boats built before the regulation went into effect probably don't have holding tanks; even if they do, the isolated anchorages that appeal to cruising yachties are not equipped with pumping stations; and even if they were, you can't necessarily count on free-spirited yachties complying with restrictions imposed by authorities ashore.

It's a problem all right, and someone had better find a solution soon. As the cruising population steadily increases, so does pollution, and this generation's yachties could easily ruin cruising for the next.

A note on heads: They're complicated. You don't just press a lever and watch the contents disappear. Instead you pump the water in, then you pump the water out, all the while manipulating valves that control the amount and the direction of the flow. There are many makes of heads, all different enough so that when visiting a yacht it is proper etiquette to inquire if there are any special instructions before using the head. Careless guests are constantly flooding and threatening to sink their friends' boats.

LAUNDRY

LAUNDRY WAS A CHORE I really hated—and spent a lot of time doing.

On a boat laundry is washed by hand, in buckets, using as little water as possible. Salt water is a no-go for laundry. I learned the hard way that things washed in seawater, even after a final rinse in fresh water, never dry completely and they seem to fade faster and rot sooner than those washed in fresh.

Unless our water jugs were all full and it was pouring rain, I used the same water over and over again, starting with the "smalls" (underwear and bikinis), on to the shirts and shorts, then the sheets and towels, and finally the dirty work clothes. This procession took most of a day, as a bucket isn't built like a washtub—it's one sheet or towel at a time.

The most efficient way to get clothes clean was to soak them while sailing on a calm day. The gentle motion of the boat was a great substitute for scrubbing. Unfortunately, I couldn't arrange a pleasant sail every time I had to do the laundry. To save my knuckles some, Peter devised a clever agitator for me, a "plumber's helper" with a few holes poked through the rubber that I plunged into the bucket over and over again.

Wringing was the hardest part. The goal was to get things as dry as possible so they would require as little rinse water as possible, but my hands weren't large or strong enough to effectively squeeze the big things. If Peter wasn't available to help with the sheets, towels and jeans, I looped them around the steering wheel, then twisted.

After rinsing in a bucket or two, I wrang again, then hung up to dry. Smalls went on the lifelines looped through their own holes, a quick and secure way to hang them.

Shorts and shirts could also go on the lifelines (the plastic-coated wires encircling the deck at thigh height) but for the bigger things we had to string a clothesline in the rigging. From the mast to the starboard shroud to the forestay to the port shroud and back to the mainmast. On a really big washday we ran lines around the mizzen mast as well. Between the tropical sun and the tradewinds, it didn't take long for the laundry to dry. I loved to watch the clothes flapping in the breeze; they seemed to dance on the lines.

If I thought we might encounter a laundromat in the foreseeable future, I saved up the big stuff and splurged on a binge of automation. After hefting sailbags full of dirty laundry ashore, I was often sorry I had. I lost a lot of detergent and coins in machines that should have been marked "out of order," and more than once our clothes were washed in recycled water and came out dirtier than they went in.

Heaven for a yachtie is to be anchored off a yacht club that has a shower and a washing machine. Most cruisers are welcome at most yacht clubs and for a nominal fee can become temporary members with use of the facilities—usually a bar, toilets and running water that might or might not include hot. There is usually a shower of some description and a place to do washing—if not a machine or tub, a tap for filling buckets.

Running water for washing clothes was irresistible. I have to confess that at a couple of yacht clubs that did welcome us for showers but did not offer laundry facilities, we smuggled dirty clothes into the showers and washed them there.

In my search for unlimited water on wash day, I also did laundry under taps at town docks where I usually attracted an audience of "wharf rats," as we called the local loiterers, or I joined the local women wherever they washed—at a well, a communal tub, a waterfall or a fresh-water stream.

It was always a pleasure to watch the women wading in a river or squatting by the side of a stream, gracefully scrubbing their clothes on stones, swishing them through the water and laying them out to dry on rocks or bushes. It certainly looked easier than dealing with my buckets on board, but I was never entirely successful at it. I lost my footing, got my soap powder wet, let smalls sink and sheets wash downstream and then got everything muddy or sandy en route from the stream to the shore.

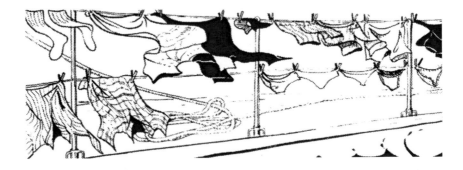

LANGUAGES

PETER LOVED LANGUAGES and picked them up easily. Wherever we went he learned how to say at least "good day" and "thank you" in the local dialect. Frequently he would acquire quite an extensive vocabulary.

My scrapbooks are full of odd bits of paper with his scribbled "dictionaries" on them. I see that in Puluwatese the word for shark is *paw* or *pa*, a sailing canoe is *waherek* and a coconut is *nu*. That knowledge was useful for exactly two weeks of our lives, the time we spent in Puluwat, a lovely atoll in the Caroline Islands. Only the 600 people who live there speak that language.

In the large island groups of the Pacific the islands are often so isolated from each other the people of one island don't necessarily speak the same language as those of the next. In fact, the people of one village don't necessarily speak the same language as the people of the other villages on the same island. They can hardly converse with each other, much less with us.

English is, luckily, the universal language of choice. Even in the most remote villages we almost always found at least one person with at least a little knowledge of English, usually the school teacher or a precocious student. If we couldn't communicate in English, we tried French, Spanish, pidgin or sign language.

Sign language, or body English, was sometimes useful but frequently dangerous. A nod that to us meant "yes" was a "no" in several cultures; our gesture for "come here" was theirs for "go away"; and a simple finger pointing the direction could be considered quite rude, even obscene, in certain places.

Pidgin English was safer and so useful in those countries with many languages that one of them, the former New Hebrides, chose a pidgin called Bislama as its official language when it became the independent country of Vanuatu.

Bislama is easy to understand, and we found it delightful to hear and read. From the local weekly newspaper, *Tam-Tam*, which was written in English, French and Bislama, we learned that the Bislama for people is *pipol*, republic is *repablik,* party is *pati*. Some favorites that became part of our personal vocabulary were *yumi* for we, *bimeby* for later and *nambawan*, meaning very good.

We attended the third Independens Selebrasen of Vanuatu in 1983, a marvelous cultural mélange. Painted ceremonial dancers from the hill tribes wore loincloths and grass skirts and stamped on the bare ground with their bare feet for two days. They were followed by a ceremony of Western-style pomp and circumstance with a uniformed brass band marching around and around, volleys of gunfire and government dignitaries in suits and ties arriving at the dais in chauffeur-driven cars to make political speeches—in Bislama.

Both Peter and I knew some French and Spanish. I had studied the two languages for years and could read them fairly well, even write them a bit, but I was hopeless at conversation; I had no "ear" for languages and I was shy about speaking imperfectly. Peter, who never studied any language formally, had picked up both of them with little effort. His grammar and pronunciation were atrocious but he wasn't the least bit self-conscious.

In the beginning I tried to correct him but soon I realized my superior education meant nothing compared to his natural ability. He communicated, and no one seemed to mind his mistakes. Even at an elegant dinner party in New Caledonia where several sailor/doctors and their wives entertained us and nothing but French was spoken, Peter was not inhibited. In fact, his tales of cruising delivered in wine-fluent French were so amusing he was the life of the party. I didn't say a word all night.

Strangely, I never presumed to correct Peter's English, which was full of "ain'ts" and "he don'ts." As an English major, a journalist and the daughter of two English teachers, I was naturally a snob about proper usage but not enough to take the chance of offending my sensitive friend. Despite his grammatical errors, it was a pleasure to listen to Peter; his accent was not of any obvious "class" or region, just nicely English, and his conversation was articulate, full of puns and refreshingly free of four-letter words. The strongest expletives I ever heard him use were "bullshit!" and "bastard!"

To understand each other, we both had to expand our English vocabularies to include the other's usage. New differences between British and American cropped up almost daily. What I called a sweater he knew as a jumper. My cookie was his biscuit, but my biscuit was his scone. What I considered the hood of a car was a bonnet to him, and my trunk was his boot. I thought homely was ugly, he thought it meant homey. When I was pissed, I was angry. When he was pissed, he was drunk.

KIDS

THERE ARE CHILDREN OF all ages aboard cruising yachts. Some sailors set out with a family. Others produce babies along the way. Cruising *en famille* is taken in stride by some yachties but for others the presence of a child signals the necessity to return to "normal" life.

Neither Peter nor I had children and we never had a child aboard for more than a brief visit, so I am certainly not an authority on juveniles afloat.

I would like to think that a child who grows up on a boat is especially privileged, and there are many parents and children who maintain that's true. I have read and heard some heartwarming stories about cruising as the ultimate in togetherness and family bonding.

I know that many children are excellent crew. And I know that when ashore, yachties with kids often have the best adventures. While adult visitors may encounter indifference, reticence or even hostility, children almost always get a warm welcome. Once they've made the entrée into local society, the rest of the family has a chance to make friends.

But back on the boat, anchored in a strange harbor for days or weeks or months, most of the children I knew were bored and unhappy. They spent most of their time in the company of adults who tried to convince them how lucky they were to live such fabulous lives—to sail the seas, visit exotic countries, meet unusual people, experience odd cultures. All true but, unfortunately, rarely appreciated at the time. Instead, the typical kid just wants to be with other kids. He misses his friends, his familiar surroundings and his junk food, and he resents his parents for making him "different." This was particularly true of the American children.

Some kids have fun in port—swimming, diving, sailing a dinghy, shelling—but unless there are siblings to play with, it is usually a lonely life. Rarely do they stay in one place long enough to make friends ashore.

Most school-age children take correspondence courses under the supervision of Mom or Dad or both, and most of the time both students and teachers find their dual roles a strain. And the hours that have to be set aside for classes and homework take quite a chunk out of everyone's day. When other yachties are working on their boats, going ashore or visiting each other, those with kids are holding school.

Younger children present fewer emotional and social problems, but they certainly create more physical ones.

With a baby or toddler aboard, parents are naturally in constant fear of his falling overboard. So most yachts with tiny tots in crew look like giant playpens, with netting stretched around the entire perimeter, from the lifelines to the decks.

Still the baby can easily come to grief, so he is stuffed into a hot, bulky life jacket, harnessed like a horse, leashed like a dog, or all of the above. Below decks, he is put to bed in a nautical version of a padded cell to protect him from injury when underway.

Some babies gurgle sweetly through all the manhandling, but most of the toddlers we met were real monsters—constantly demanding attention, screaming relentlessly and throwing frequent tantrums. I naturally concluded that there seemed to be a direct correlation between boat life and problem children.

PETS

I'M AN ANIMAL LOVER but, in my opinion, pets are pests on a cruising yacht. Cats are better than dogs because they don't need to be exercised and they are happy to do their business in a litter box. But who wants to sail around with a stinky box full of pee and poo!

We met some other sailing pets in our travels: a cockatoo which, despite its clipped wings, kept trying to fly and had to be fished out of the water regularly; and a marmoset, a mean raucous South American critter of the monkey family, who had to be kept in a cage. But most ship's mascots were not exotic. They were simply cats or dogs their owners couldn't bear to leave behind when they set off cruising.

Peter had a dog named Mr. Wags, a medium-sized mutt, mostly collie, with a tail like a question mark. Peter acquired him in England as a puppy, and they had a classic man-and-his-dog relationship. The "Mister" designated Wags as a ship's officer. In fact he was considered first mate.

When I joined the crew of *Solanderi*, I was jealous of the dog. But I grew to accept his place in Peter's affections and even to love him myself. He was a super dog.

Peter had him beautifully trained. He didn't even own a leash. If Wags just looked as if he'd like to do something naughty, Peter simply had to say, very quietly, "Mind your manners, Mr. Wags," and he would.

Peter took Wags everywhere—to other boats, to people's homes, to restaurants, to stores. He just assumed that such a perfect dog would be welcome anywhere. He was quite surprised and offended if we weren't allowed in.

When we were in port, Peter took Wags ashore for "walkies" every morning and evening. But when we were at sea, the dog really suffered. Although there was plenty of deck space where he could "go" and he was urged to use the port bow, he preferred to hold everything until he burst. After about 48 hours he finally let go, but right away he started saving up again.

That wasn't Mr. Wag's only problem. Peter wouldn't admit it, but sailing made the poor dog a nervous wreck, more and more as he grew older. When we tacked, the flapping sails sent him flying down the companionway into the salon, where he crawled under the table into his security corner and trembled. He was never really happy until he heard the outboard motor start. That, he knew, meant we were entering a harbor. He clambered up the ladder to the deck, ran to the bows and sniffed the land deliriously. Then he ran circles around the deck until the anchor was finally down. Poor Peter—both Wags and I considered dropping the anchor the best part of a sailing trip.

Mr. Wags was never "fixed." The older he got, the more interested he became in sex. During our last couple of years in

Tortola, he frequently took off for three or four days at a time whenever he sniffed a bitch in heat. When he came home, starved and exhausted, covered with cuts and bruises, he lay on deck for days, barely able to lick his wounds.

The last time we saw him he was hot on the trail again. When he never returned, we had to assume he had been shot or poisoned, the usual fate of a dog that makes a nuisance of himself in the islands.

The only alternative was that, being a friendly dog who never refused a handout and who felt at home on any boat, he might have been lured aboard another yacht and spirited away.

Whatever happened, his disappearance had its bright side. We were finally really getting ready to go to the Pacific where almost every country had strict quarantine laws; all animals had to be kept on board for six months. Wags would have found that unacceptable. Maybe he had a whiff of the future when he decided to abandon ship.

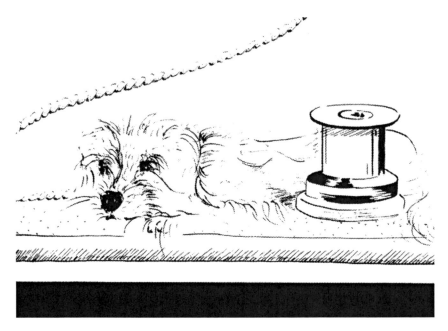

THIEVES AND PIRATES

IN ALL OUR YEARS OF CRUISING, we rarely locked the boat. We spent most of our time in idyllic places where theft hardly ever happened to a yacht and we felt perfectly safe leaving the boat wide open, even though everything we owned was aboard.

What a shock, when we entered the South China Sea, to hear the tales of theft and piracy and to see the yachts equipped with burglar alarms and electric cattle fences!

In the Philippines, theft was epidemic. Just before we arrived, in 1985, there was a rash of burglaries on yachts. They happened in the middle of the night—while the owners slept. We heard one unbelievable tale after another of yachties waking up in the morning to find they had been robbed of everything. Electronic gear had been

143

ripped out of the cabins where they were sleeping. Anchors and chains had been removed from the decks above them. On one memorable night about a dozen yachts in one anchorage were completely cleaned out.

Most sailors pride themselves on their ability to sense things in their sleep; a wind shift or a slight change in the boat's motion will have them on deck in a flash. How, then, could they not realize that someone was aboard? How on earth could they fail to hear, say, 50 feet of ¾-inch chain leaving the boat?

The victims were sure they hadn't been knocked out or gassed. There were no bruises, no headaches or hangovers, except for the usual alcoholic ones.

To my knowledge, the mystery was never solved.

Despite the frightening stories, Peter wanted to go to the Philippines, but he took the precaution of installing an alarm system on *Solanderi* first. The minute a hatch was opened a switch was tripped that set off a siren and strobe light on top of the mast. We activated the system whenever we left the boat and when we went to bed.

The only problem was, we still chose to sleep on deck rather than sweat in a closed-up cabin below, and a prospective burglar would see us or trip over us before he got to the hatch that triggered the alarm. We were comforted to hear that Filipino burglars rarely inflicted bodily harm. Nevertheless, I didn't sleep too well.

Most of the Filipinos we met were good-natured, fun-loving nice guys, just like the people we had enjoyed all over the Pacific. But now we could no longer assume that everyone was friendly.

In fact, I was terrified of every *banca* that approached us. The local boats are spooky-looking craft—long, thin canoes with two outriggers attached by bowed arms that look like spider legs. They

were often propelled by a fast outboard motor and always full of men. They would turn out to be a bunch of fishermen just looking us over, laughing and waving, but I had lost that wonderful trust in people. They were all potential pirates now.

From the Philippines we were planning to cruise through Borneo, Malaysia and Thailand en route to the Indian Ocean. Cruising lore was full or horror stories about pirates in those countries. Particularly in the Strait of Malacca, the narrow strip of water between Malaysia and Sumatra, attacks on yachts were frequent. The pirates were said to have no respect for human life. They killed the people to get the boat.

Cruising suddenly lost its charm for me, and I didn't see much hope of getting it back. If I managed to survive the pirates, my next few years would be spent sailing across the huge Indian Ocean, with only a few small islands on the way; then rounding the Cape of Good Hope, one of the roughest passages in the world; and finally crossing the Atlantic, to complete the circumnavigation.

I couldn't do it. After 12 mostly idyllic years of sailing halfway around the world with a man I adored, I finally had to admit I couldn't do what he was doing anymore. I had to quit.

Leaving Peter and our life together was my toughest trip ever, but fear had finally won out over love.

145

I packed all my possessions in two tiny duffel bags and, badly torn between relief and regret, flew away. In less than a day I was back where I started.

—THE END—

POSTSCRIPT

I "buried the anchor" on a hillside in St. Croix, Virgin Islands, where I designed and built my dream house overlooking the Caribbean Sea. I love it from afar.

Peter stayed in the Philippines, sold Solanderi *and designed and built his dream boat. He married and had a daughter and they all sailed on.*

Emy Thomas

Emy Thomas

ABOUT THE AUTHOR

Emy Thomas grew up in Connecticut, was educated at prestigious schools in the northeast, and worked as a journalist in New York City. Then she discovered the tropics and has embraced the islands and their laid-back lifestyle ever since. After her 13-year adventure at sea, she settled on St. Croix in the U.S. Virgin Islands, where she lives and writes overlooking the Caribbean Sea. Her second book, *Life in the Left Lane*, is about the lifestyle of expatriates in the islands, especially St. Croix.

CPSIA information can be obtained at www.ICGtesting.com
Printed in the USA
BVOW031607290512

291299BV00001B/2/A